EAT WELL ON $4/DAY

GOOD
AND
CHEAP

LEANNE BROWN

W9-API-133

First, I'd like to thank my husband, Dan. Without him this book would not exist. Thank you also to my wonderful family and friends, who believed in this idea before anyone else. And thank you to everyone who has taken the time to tell me what *Good and Cheap* means to them. I heard from thousands of people throughout the course of creating and distributing this book. The outpouring of love and support I've received is probably enough for several lifetimes. To those who told me this book has given them hope, inspired them, or otherwise brought them pleasure: I don't deserve so much gratitude for so little, but doing work that matters is all I have ever wanted.

Text, recipes, and most photographs and design by Leanne Brown, in fulfillment of a final project for a master's degree in Food Studies at New York University.

Editing and some photographs and design by my husband, Dan Lazin.

This book is distributed under a Creative Commons Attribution-NonCommercialShareAlike 4.0 license. For more information, visit www.creativecommons.org/licenses/by-nc-sa/4.0

You may freely distribute this book electronically. To download a free PDF or buy a print copy, visit www.leannebrown.com

Brown, Leanne
Good and Cheap: Eat Well on $4/Day
ISBN: 978-0-9938448-1-1

Printed in the United States of America

Version 1.1, September 2014
Version 1.0, June 2014
Version 0.9, December 2013

Introduction

Eating is one of life's greatest pleasures. In a perfect world, healthy and delicious food would be all around us. It would be easy to choose and easy to enjoy.

But of course it's not a perfect world. There are thousands of barriers that can keep us from eating in a way that nourishes our bodies and satisfies our tastes. Money just needn't be one of them.

Kitchen skill, not budget, is the key to great food. This cookbook is a celebration of the many delicious meals available to those on even the most strict of budgets.

Eating on a limited budget is not easy, and there are times when a tough week can turn mealtime into a chore. As one woman told me, "I'm weary of the 'what's for dinner?' game." I hope the recipes and techniques in this book can help make those times rare and the tough choices a little more bearable.

At the same time, this book is not a meal plan—those are much too individual to share on a wide scale. Every person and every family has specific needs and unique tastes. We live in different regions, different neighborhoods, and with varying means. One book cannot account for all of that, but I hope it can be a spark, a general strategy, a flexible set of approachable and cheap recipes. The rest is up to you.

I think you'll find (or perhaps have already found) that learning to cook has a powerfully positive effect. If you can become a more skilled, more conscious cook, you'll be able to conjure deliciousness in any kitchen, anytime. Good cooking alone can't solve hunger in America, but it can make life happier—and that is worth every effort.

Just as a good meal is best shared with others, so is a good recipe. I may not be able to share a meal with you, but I'd love to offer a few ideas. What's for dinner? Here's my answer.

A Note on $4/Day

I designed these recipes to fit the budgets of people living on SNAP, the US program that used to be called food stamps. If you're on SNAP, you already know that the benefit formulas are complicated, but the rule of thumb is that you end up with $4 per person, per day to spend on food.

This book isn't challenging you to live on so little; it's a resource in case that's your reality. In May 2014, there were 46 million Americans on food stamps. Untold millions more—in particular, retirees and students—live under similar constraints.

The costs for each recipe are based on two sources. For the pantry items on the following pages, I collected prices from four grocery stores in Inwood, a relatively low-income neighborhood on the north tip of Manhattan. For specific spices and a wider variety of fruits and vegetables, I looked at online grocery stores or nationwide averages collected by the Bureau of Labor Statistics.

The prices for fruits and vegetables assume that they're roughly in season, when you can get the best deals. This means, unfortunately, that you'll pay a lot more if you want to make peach coffee cake in February. I talk more about shopping in season on the following pages.

The estimates are, by necessity, a snapshot of place and time. Costs will vary in other cities, other neighborhoods, even just other stores. Please think of the numbers as a guideline, not a guarantee.

More than in most cookbooks, my recipes are flexible and encourage substitution based on availability, price, and personal tastes. A strict budget requires flexibility and a willingness to say, "that's a good deal this week, so it's what I'll be cooking!" Don't worry, you'll pick up the tricks quickly.

A few recipes call for fancy kitchen equipment, but in my work with low-income families in New York, I've found that items like blenders, food processors, and electric mixers are fairly common. I did not, however, attempt to tackle the very real situation of people who have no kitchen, no equipment, and no space to prepare food. I simply cannot hope to do those issues justice within the bounds of one cookbook. Let's all agree that we need to keep striving to address those other issues that make it difficult for so many people to eat well.

My Philosophy

The best health advice is simple: eat fruits and vegetables. Many American cookbooks rely on meat as the central feature of a meal. My recipes celebrate the vegetables rather than the meat.

My intent was to create satisfying food that doesn't require you to supplement your meals with cheap carbohydrates to stave off hunger. I strove to create recipes that use money *carefully*, without being purely slavish to the bottom line. For example, many recipes use butter rather than oil. Butter is not cheap, but it creates flavor, crunch, and richness in a way that cheap oils never can.

I'm not a dietician, and this isn't a diet book. I'm just a home cook, like you. If you have dietary restrictions, some recipes won't work for you as-is, but that's fine—you can try to adapt them to your needs, or just turn the page and keep looking for inspiration.

More than a book of recipes, this is a book of ideas. I *want* you to tailor things to your taste. Improvisation is the soul of great cooking! If it doesn't work out every time, I hope you'll forgive me. More importantly, forgive yourself, and try again.

About this Book

I created an earlier version of this book as the capstone project for my MA in Food Studies at New York University. After I posted a free PDF on my website, it went viral on Reddit, Tumblr, and elsewhere, racking up almost 100,000 downloads in the first few weeks. That support gave me the courage to launch a Kickstarter campaign to get printed copies of *Good and Cheap* into the hands of people who don't have computers or who wouldn't otherwise see it. Thousands of generous supporters contributed to the campaign, donating more than 8,000 free copies of the printed book and sponsoring 20 new recipes. Now, just five months after first posting the PDF, it has been downloaded about 500,000 times.

The experience has changed my life.

Tips for Eating and Shopping Well

BUY FOODS THAT CAN BE USED IN MULTIPLE MEALS

Versatile ingredients save meals. If you buy flour, you can make tortillas (p. 137), roti (p. 138), scones (p. 22), and pancakes (p. 18). If you buy yogurt (or make your own), you can have it with fruit (p. 32), make raita (p. 164) and tzatziki (p. 165), or use it in a drink (p. 150). Need I even mention the versatility of garlic or lemons? If you always keep them around, you can make anything else taste fantastic.

BUY IN BULK

Buying larger amounts usually brings the price down. When you're working within a tight budget, you won't always be able to afford to shop for the future, but do it when you can. And, of course, keep storage in mind: If the item will go off before you can finish it, get the smaller size. If you buy versatile ingredients in slightly larger amounts, you'll be able to use them quickly but still make diverse meals.

START BUILDING A PANTRY

If possible—and admittedly this can be difficult for people living on their own—reserve part of your budget to buy one or two semi-expensive pantry items each week. Things like olive oil, soy sauce, and spices (p. 166) are pricey at first, but if you use just a little with each recipe, they go a long way. With turmeric, coriander, cumin, and fresh ginger root, you'll suddenly have a world of flavor on your shelf. In a few pages, I'll suggest specific items to add to your pantry.

THINK WEEKLY

Each week, mix things up by buying different varieties of staple foods like grains and beans. This week, you might have oatmeal every morning (p. 28) with black bean chili or black bean tacos later in the day, but next week you'll have yogurt for breakfast (p. 32) and hummus or chana masala (p. 93) for lunch and dinner. If you have time to shop frequently, pick up smaller amounts of produce every couple of days to ensure everything is fresh. It's a lot more inspiring to pull crisp greens out of the fridge than to unstick a wilted mess from the bottom of the veggie drawer. If you can't shop as often, consider getting canned or frozen versions of whichever vegetables you won't use immediately.

THINK SEASONALLY

During their local growing season, fruits and vegetables are generally cheaper and definitely tastier than outside of season. You'll notice that orange prices shoot up during the summer, yet what's available is drab and flavorless. But oranges are abundant in December and January, the peak of their season, and that's reflected in the price. At the end of summer, you can get bags of zucchini for next to nothing. Brussels sprouts are also very seasonal, coming on sale around Thanksgiving. Enjoy as much of the summer and fall produce as possible, because you'll be more limited in the winter. Then again, simmering and roasting winter vegetables is a fine way to warm up your house, and tough winter roots are easy to store. In addition, winter is a great time to search for deals on canned and frozen produce. Seasons for fruits and vegetables vary depending on where you live, so consult a local guide to growing seasons and use it to shop for the best deals.

MORE VEGETABLES MEANS MORE FLAVOR

Nothing livens up a bowl of rice like summer squash and corn! Vegetables make the best sauces: they're earthy, bright, tart, sweet, bitter, savory, rich. Give them a treasured spot at the top of your grocery list and you'll never be bored.

More Tips!

ALWAYS BUY EGGS

With these babies in your fridge, you're only minutes away from a satisfying meal. Scramble an egg with leftovers or drop an egg on top of a salad or a plate of stir-fried vegetables, and deliciousness is guaranteed.

BUY EXPENSIVE EGGS IF YOU CAN

More expensive eggs are usually worth the money—they taste so much better than cheap eggs. Even at $4 a dozen, you're still only paying 33 cents an egg. Really fresh eggs, like those from a farmers' market, also make a big difference in flavor.

BE CAREFUL WITH UNDERCOOKED EGGS

Very rarely, raw eggs can be infected with salmonella. Many classic recipes, from mayonnaise to eggnog to Caesar dressing, are prepared with raw egg yolk, but technically only a hard-cooked egg is guaranteed to be free of salmonella. Consequently, raw or runny eggs are not recommended for infants, the elderly, pregnant women, or anyone with a weakened immune system.

BUY FRESH BREAD

Try to buy fresh loaves of interesting bread from an independent bakery or the bakery in your grocery store. Although fresh loaves don't last as long as sliced bread, they're much more enjoyable, and you can use the old stuff to make panzanella (p. 49) or croutons or breadcrumbs (p. 146) to top other dishes. Later in the day, many independent bakeries offer deep discounts on bread they would otherwise have to throw out.

DON'T BUY DRINKS

All the body needs drink-wise is water. Except for milk, most packaged drinks are overpriced and deliver a lot of sugar without filling you up the way a piece of fruit or a bowl of yogurt does. If you want a special drink, make agua fresca (p. 149), a smoothie (p. 150), or tea.

GET CREATIVE WITH WILTED VEGETABLES

Sometimes you forget a pepper or bunch of spinach in the back of the fridge. Although wilted veggies might not remain fit for a salad, they'll still be wonderful in any dish that calls for sautéed, grated, or baked vegetables. Just cut off any actual rot. You can also use them in broth.

MAKE YOUR OWN BROTH AND STOCK

In almost any savory recipe that calls for water, homemade broth or stock would be better. To make broth, start by saving any vegetable bits that you chop off and would normally throw away, like onion tops, the seedy parts of peppers, and the ends of carrots. Store them in the freezer until you have a few cups, then cover them with water, bring to a boil, and simmer on low heat for a few hours. Add salt to taste, and you have broth! To make a hearty stock, do the same with leftover bones or scraps of meat (preferably all the same kind of meat). Since you're using stuff you'd otherwise throw away, broth and stock are effectively free.

TREAT YOUR FREEZER WITH RESPECT

A freezer can be a great friend for saving time by letting you prepare large batches of food at once. Cooking dried beans takes a while (p. 145), so make more than you need, then freeze the rest. Another great trick I learned from a reader is to dice a whole package of bacon, fry it, then freeze it in small parcels. This makes it easy to add a small amount of bacon to a dish without the temptation of using the whole package.

TURN CHICKEN SKIN INTO SCHMALTZ

Schmaltz is rendered chicken fat that you can use like butter. Buy chicken that still has its skin, then trim the skins and lay them in a pan on low heat. Add a cup or so of water and simmer until the fat releases from the skin and the water cooks off. Let the fat cool, then throw away the skins and pour the fat into a glass jar. Store in the fridge.

BUY A PEPPER GRINDER

Seriously, banish pre-ground pepper from your life; it loses all flavor when it sits around. Fresh pepper creates pops of intense flavor on the tongue and lights up bland dishes. One of the most popular dishes in Rome is just pasta with butter and pepper: give it a try!

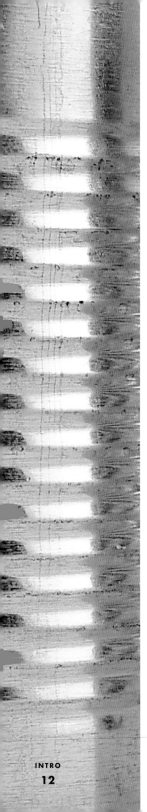
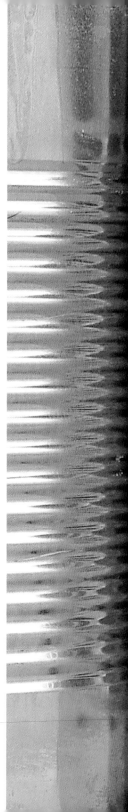

Pantry Basics

With these commonly available items in your pantry, you can have a wide variety of meals on the table within minutes. Keeping a well stocked pantry is the key to easy, fast cooking at home. When you're living on a budget, building up supplies does take time, but just keep adding each week and you'll get there in time.

VEGETABLES

Vegetables can (and should!) be the base of most meals. Other than greens, which should be used quickly, these can be stored for a few days to a few weeks. Try each vegetable as it hits peak season and goes on sale.

garlic, onions, carrots, celery, peppers, broccoli, tomatoes, hot peppers, hardy greens, salad greens, potatoes, sweet potatoes, cauliflower, winter squash

FRUITS

Citrus fruits are cooking essentials and they keep well. The zest and juice can liven up just about any dish and they always make a great dressing. Bananas, apples, and melons are great quick snacks, but try every fruit you can afford! Remember, almost all fruits and vegetables have a season, so savor them at their freshest and cheapest.

apples, melons, oranges, limes, lemons, bananas

DAIRY

Butter is just as good to cook with as it is on toast. These are the cheeses I like, but buy what your taste, budget, and local availability alllow.

butter, milk, yogurt, queso fresco, Romano or Parmesan, sharp cheddar, mozzarella

PROTEIN

Meat isn't the only protein! The items below are cheap, easily stored, and have multiple uses. Be aware that most fish at the grocery store has previously been frozen and was merely thawed for display. There's no harm in buying it frozen and thawing it yourself.

eggs, dried beans, lentils, tofu, nuts, peanut butter

GRAINS

Flour is so inexpensive, and once you have a few basics at hand, most baked goods are a cinch to make. There's great variety in whole grains. Substitute them for rice, toss them in a salad, or add them to soup.

bread, tortillas, pasta, all-purpose flour, whole-wheat flour, oats, popcorn, short-grain rice, long-grain rice, brown rice, cornmeal, dried whole grains

CANNED VEGETABLES

Plenty of vegetables are good when canned, so remember to compare prices between fresh, frozen, and canned. The canned versions are fantastic in sauces. Just be aware that canned foods are often very salty, so you might want to rinse them, except for canned tomatoes.

whole tomatoes, tomato paste, whole corn

FROZEN FRUITS AND VEGETABLES

Fresh berries can be expensive, but the frozen ones often go on sale and are great for smoothies. Frozen veggies are quick to add to soups and rice dishes. Again, compare prices to see whether frozen is the best value.

berries, peas, green beans, corn

FLAVOR AND COOKING

You can explore an extraordinary number of cuisines with these items. They add depth and excitement to the most simple dishes.

olive oil or vegetable oil, wine vinegar, anchovies, sardines, olives, fish sauce, coconut milk, miso paste, mustard, soy sauce, chili sauce, brown sugar, fresh herbs, dried spices (p. 166)

TREATS THAT GO A LONG WAY

Although these items can be expensive, a little goes a long way; when you can, pick up an item or two and enjoy the results.

dried fruits, dried mushrooms, frozen shrimp, maple syrup, bacon, vanilla, cocoa powder

SPICES

I have a whole page on spices (p. 166), but they can be a sticking point: no food value, and they sometimes have a high sticker price. However, one small bottle lasts many meals, so invest in them whenever you can.

Breakfast

Fast, healthy, and cheap is usually the game plan for breakfast—with as much pleasing flavor as I can manage in my grouchy morning state. Whether you have hours or minutes, there's a great breakfast to be had for little.

Tomato Scrambled Eggs

FOR TWO

$3.60 TOTAL
$1.80 / SERVING

For today's breakfast, fluffy, creamy eggs hold together a mass of tangy, juicy, sweet tomatoes. Best enjoyed when tomatoes are in season.

½ tbsp butter

4 cups fresh tomatoes or 2 cups canned tomatoes, chopped

4 eggs

salt and pepper

ADDITIONS

fresh basil or other herbs, chopped

Put a small pan on medium heat and melt the butter, then swirl it around to coat the pan. Add the tomatoes. Cook until the tomatoes release their juice and most of the juice evaporates, about 5 to 7 minutes.

Meanwhile, crack the eggs into a bowl and add a generous sprinkling of salt and pepper. Beat the eggs lightly with a fork.

Once most of the juice has cooked out of the tomatoes, turn the heat down to low and add the eggs to the pan. Using a spatula, gently mix the eggs and tomatoes. Carefully stir the eggs to keep them from forming chunks. Turn down the heat as low as possible; the slower your eggs cook, the creamier they'll be.

Once the eggs are done, turn off the heat and add any chopped herbs you have around. Basil is the best with tomatoes.

If you have some around, serve over toast or a tortilla.

$2 TOTAL
$1 / SERVING

Broiled Grapefruit

FOR TWO

If your oven has a broiler, this is a fast and fun way to liven up a standard, healthy breakfast of grapefruit. This method produces a hot and sticky treat.

2 grapefruit
2 tbsp brown sugar
salt

Turn on the broiler in your oven.

Split a grapefruit in half and place it on a baking tray or in an oven-proof pan. Sprinkle the pink halves evenly with sugar and top with just a tiny bit of salt to bring out the flavor.

Place the grapefruit halves under the broiler until they turn bubbly and a little brown (or even black) around the edges. This usually takes about 3 minutes, but monitor it because every broiler is different. Don't get distracted! Overbroiling ruins a good meal fast.

If you have maple syrup on hand, use it instead of sugar for even more flavor.

This breakfast will make a grapefruit lover out of you!

$1.60 TOTAL
$0.80 / SERVING

Omelette

FOR TWO

I make this omelette at least once a week. It's insanely delicious, whether laden with veggies or kept simple. I love it with dill, but it's good with almost any herb or scallions. Once you are a pro at making this, add any other cooked veggies you have around.

4 eggs
2 tbsp fresh dill, finely chopped
salt and pepper
butter for the pan
1 shallot or ½ small red onion, finely diced
¼ cup grated cheese

Crack the eggs in a bowl. Add the dill, salt, pepper, and beat with a fork.

Put a big saucepan on medium-high heat. Melt a small blob of butter in the pan. Once the butter is sizzling, add the onion and sauté for about two minutes, until it's translucent and smells great.

Add the egg to the hot pan and swirl it around to coat the surface evenly. If the center of the omelette cooks more quickly than the edge, use a spatula to pull any raw egg into the middle. Then stop touching it.

After about 30 seconds, toss the cheese on top along with any other raw or cooked vegetable you feel like adding. Once none of the egg remains translucent, fold the omelette in half with your spatula, then lift it out of the pan. You don't want any brown on your eggs.

If I'm serving two people, I usually cut one large omelette in half rather than making two omelettes. However, when you feel like being fancy, you can make a pair of two-egg omelettes simply by using half the ingredients for each. For extra fanciness, roll up the omelette instead of folding it—that's how the French do it, traditionally. The result will be quite thin and tender.

Banana Pancakes

MAKES TEN TO FOURTEEN PANCAKES

With the creamy texture and delicious flavor of bananas, these pancakes are stunningly good. You will be seriously popular if you feed these to your family or friends. Another plus: this is a great way to get rid of mushy bananas (that doesn't involve making banana bread).

2 cups all-purpose flour
¼ cup brown sugar
2 tsp baking powder
1 tsp baking soda
1 tsp salt
2 bananas, mashed
2 eggs
1½ cups milk
1 tsp vanilla
2 bananas, sliced
butter for cooking

In a medium bowl, add the flour, brown sugar, baking powder, soda and salt. Mix thoroughly with a spoon.

In another bowl, add the mashed bananas (or just mash them in the bowl), eggs, milk, and vanilla, then mix. Add the dry mixture from the other bowl into the second bowl. Gently stir it with a spoon until everything just comes together. Tender pancakes come from not over-mixing the batter. If there are still a few pockets of flour, don't worry about it. Let the mixture sit for 10 to 15 minutes.

Place a non-stick or cast-iron pan on medium heat. Once it's hot, melt a small amount of butter, about ½ teaspoon, then ladle some pancake batter into the center of the pan. You can make your pancakes as large or small as you like. A normal amount is about ¼ to ⅓ cup of batter. If it's your first time making pancakes, make them smaller: they'll be easier to flip.

As soon as the batter is in the pan, place 3 to 4 banana slices atop of the uncooked side of the pancake. Once the edges of the pancake start to dry up and you can see the middle start to bubble, flip the pancake over. Cook until it is browned on both sides. Stack the finished pancake on a plate in a warm oven and repeat the above process until you run out of batter.

Serve hot, with butter and syrup.

$2.80 TOTAL
$0.70 / SERVING

$4.80 TOTAL
$0.20 / MUFFIN

Chocolate Zucchini Muffins

MAKES TWENTY-FOUR SMALL MUFFINS

2 cups grated zucchini
1½ cups all-purpose flour
1½ cups oats
½ cup cocoa powder
1½ cups sugar
1 tbsp cinnamon (optional)
2 tsp baking soda
1 tsp salt
4 eggs
1 cup plain yogurt
½ cup dark chocolate chips (optional)

When my friend Michael challenged me to create a recipe that used dark chocolate, I got a little worried: dark chocolate is expensive!

But then I remembered that cocoa powder is deeply, darkly chocolaty, without the expense. I thought of the chocolate zucchini cake my mother made when I was growing up and knew I had something.

This is a great breakfast treat that uses staples you should generally have on hand like flour, oats, and yogurt. The yogurt and zucchini make these muffins super moist and yummy, but still a reasonably nutritious (if slightly sugary) choice for breakfast.

Make these in mid-summer, during the height of zucchini season, when larger zucchini are really cheap. Big zucchini are generally a bit woodier, but they're still great for baking.

Preheat the oven to 350 °F.

Cut off the round end of the zucchini (which is a little tough), but keep the stem to use as a handhold. Shred the zucchini with a box grater, stopping when you get to the stem.

Butter or oil 24 muffin tins, or just line them with muffin cups.

Measure the dry ingredients (flour, oats, cocoa powder, sugar, cinnamon, baking soda, and salt) into a medium bowl.

Mix the zucchini, eggs, and yogurt in a larger bowl. Add the dry ingredients, then mix until everything is just combined. Add the chocolate chips if you're using them, then stir once.

With a spoon, dollop the batter into the muffin tins until each cup is about ¾ full and bake for 20 minutes.

Pull the muffins out and poke with a toothpick or knife. If it comes out wet, bake the muffins for 5 more minutes.

Let the muffins cool in their tins for 20 to 30 minutes, then eat them warm!

Whole-Wheat Jalapeño Cheddar Scones

MAKES SIX

These are delicious for breakfast or with a plate of beans, a pile of vegetables, or alongside a chili or stew. Spicy, cheesy, flaky—these are best eaten straight out of the oven.

½ cup butter
2½ cups whole-wheat flour
1 tbsp baking powder
1 tsp salt
4 oz sharp cheddar, diced
1 jalapeño, finely diced
2 eggs, lightly beaten
½ cup milk

EGG WASH
1 egg
salt and pepper

Place the butter in the freezer for 30 minutes.

Turn the oven to 400 °F. Line a baking sheet with parchment paper, or lightly grease the pan if you don't have the paper.

In a large bowl, combine the flour, baking powder, and salt.

Prepare your jalapeño and cheese. Cutting the cheese into cubes rather than grating it means you'll have pockets of gooey cheese that contrast nicely with the scone. If you want the spice of the jalapeño, leave the seeds and membrane; if you like it milder, remove them and chop up only the pepper itself.

Remove the butter from the freezer and grate it directly into the flour mixture. (Use a cheese grater—it's the best way to break up butter without melting it.) Using your hands, gently squish the butter into the flour until everything is incorporated but not smooth. The chunks of butter will create flaky scones. Add the jalapeño, cheese, eggs, and milk to the bowl, then use your hands to gently mix everything until it just comes together. It will probably be a little shaggy, but that's just fine.

Sprinkle flour on a clean countertop and dump the dough onto it. Gently shape the dough into a disc about 1½" thick. Cut the dough into six triangles, like a pizza, and move them to the cookie sheet.

In a small bowl, gently beat the egg for the egg wash. Brush it over the scones, then sprinkle salt and pepper over each one. Bake for 25 minutes or until the scones are golden brown.

$4.50 TOTAL
$0.75 / SCONE

$3.60 TOTAL
$0.30 / BAR

Peanut Butter and Jelly Granola Bars

MAKES TWELVE

Heat the oven to 350 °F.

Butter or oil an 8" x 11" baking pan. If you have a different size pan, that's fine—it'll just change how thick the bars are.

Pour the oats into a large bowl. You can use quick oats if they're all you have, but I prefer the bite and chew of rolled oats. For a different texture, you can also substitute a cup of oats with a cup of Rice Krispies, but the bars are great either way.

Add the peanut butter, half the jelly, the water, and the salt to a small pan. Stir over low heat until it's smooth.

Mix the peanut butter and jelly concoction into the oats until all the oats are coated and you have a sticky mass. Dump the mixture into the oiled pan and press it into an even layer. Spread the remaining jelly over the top.

Pop the pan into the oven for 25 minutes, until it's toasty and brown around the edges. Mmm. Crunchy.

Leave the bars in the pan until they cool completely, about an hour, then slice into 12 bars.

Tired of endless PB+J sandwiches? Give these bars a try instead! I designed them for my friend Alex, who is allergic to gluten and is the best long-distance runner I know. I wanted to create a simple but nutritious breakfast that he could grab on his way out for a run. They are a little more crumbly than a store-bought granola bar, however.

As a bonus, these are made entirely from ingredients that you can find in any corner store or food pantry. Any kind of jam or jelly will do; I used blueberry, but grape or strawberry or any other flavor would be tasty.

3 cups rolled oats (or 2 cups oats and 1 cup Rice Krispies)
½ cup peanut butter
½ cup jelly or jam
¼ cup hot water
¼ tsp salt
butter or vegetable oil

ADDITIONS

nuts
coconut
dried fruit
honey

Egg Sandwich with Mushroom Hash

FOR TWO

Egg sandwiches are a mainstay of every corner deli in NYC, and for good reason: they're cheap and easy, fast and delicious. I knew I had to include one when Charlene, one of my early supporters, asked for a recipe with eggs and mushrooms. (I'm thankful she did! Because I don't really like mushrooms, they're scarce in this book, even though plenty of people love them.) Like most sandwiches, this recipe is really flexible. In particular, you can change the hash to use whatever you have around. Sad leftovers can take on new life when turned into a hash and matched with the rich fattiness of a morning egg.

2 tsp butter
1 small potato, diced
½ lb mushrooms, sliced
2 cloves garlic, finely chopped
2 eggs
  salt and pepper
2 rolls, 2 English muffins,
  or 4 slices of bread

ADDITIONS
tomato, sliced
avocado
cheese

VARIATIONS
potato and onion
potato and pea
collards and bacon
zucchini
chorizo and green chili

Melt half the butter in a pan on medium heat, then throw in the potato and cook for 5 minutes, stirring minimally. Season with salt and pepper. Add the mushrooms and garlic, as well as a splash of water if the potatoes are getting stuck to the pan. Cook for another 5 minutes, until the mushrooms are brown and have shrunk down.

Test the potato by piercing one piece with a fork. If it goes through easily, you're done. If not, cook for a few more minutes. (The smaller the potatoes are chopped, the quicker they'll cook.) Taste and adjust the seasoning to your preferences.

Melt the other teaspoon of butter in another pan on medium heat. Crack the eggs into the pan and dust with salt and pepper again. Salt and pepper are critical to these ingredients, so don't worry about overdoing it.

If you like your eggs sunny-side up, place a lid over the pan to ensure the whites will cook through without making the yolks hard. Once the whites are no longer translucent, take them off the heat.

If you like eggs over-easy (my favorite), wait until the yolks are cooked but still look runny, then flip each egg with a spatula and let the other side cook for about 15 seconds. That'll get your whites fully cooked, but keep the yolks runny—the best. If you prefer hard yolks (please no!), then cook for a little longer.

Toast the bread or bun, then assemble it into a sandwich, using any condiments you like. Way better than what you'll find at the corner deli.

$3.60 TOTAL
$1.80 / SANDWICH

$0.25 TOTAL
$0.13 / SERVING

Oatmeal

This basic recipe can be dressed up in so many ways, you'll never get bored. Oatmeal makes a hot and comforting breakfast; it'll give you energy for a great morning. It's also extremely inexpensive, so you can spend a bit more on lunch and dinner.

1 cup rolled oats
2 cups water
¼ tsp salt

In a small pot, add the oats, water and salt. Place it on medium-high heat, just until the water comes to a boil. Immediately turn the heat to low and place a lid on the pot. Cook for 5 minutes, until the oats are soft and tender and most of the water has cooked off. You can add more water if you like your oatmeal smooth and thin, or use slightly less if you want a thick oatmeal.

This is just the basic recipe; several ideas for how to make it your own follow on the next pages. Whether it's milky and sweet or savory and salty, I'm sure you can find a favorite way to enjoy a hot bowl of oats in the morning!

COCONUT AND LIME OATMEAL: Add the coconut and sugar to the oatmeal, water, and salt. Cook as normal. Turn off the heat and squeeze the juice of half a lime over the top.

¼ cup coconut, shredded
2 tbsp sugar
½ lime, juiced

$1.50 TOTAL
$0.75 / SERVING

BERRY OATMEAL: Cook the oatmeal as usual, but 2 minutes before it's ready, add some fresh or frozen berries and the sugar, then stir to combine. There's nothing more to the recipe than that, but it's surprising how many variations you can come up with just by trying a new type of berry or combining several varieties.

½ cup berries, fresh or frozen
1 tbsp sugar

$1.10 TOTAL
$0.55 / SERVING

$1.50 TOTAL
$0.75 / SERVING

PUMPKIN OATMEAL: Whisk the pumpkin, milk, and water in a pot. Add the oats, salt, sugar, and spices, but use just 1¼ cups water. Cook on medium-low until it bubbles. Turn to low for 5 more minutes. Add syrup or more sugar to taste.

½ cup canned pumpkin
¾ cup milk (or almond / soy milk)
1¼ cups water
2 tbsp brown sugar
1 tsp cinnamon

OPTIONAL

¼ tsp ginger powder
¼ tsp clove powder
maple syrup

$1.50 TOTAL
$0.75 / SERVING

BAKLAVA OATMEAL: Before cooking the oatmeal as normal, add the cinnamon, orange zest and 2 tablespoons of honey. Once it's cooked, top each bowl with another tablespoon of honey and a tablespoon of nuts.

1 tsp cinnamon
1 tbsp orange zest, finely grated
4 tbsp honey
2 tbsp almonds or pistachios, chopped

APPLE CINNAMON OATMEAL: Cook the oats in juice and cinnamon instead of water. Top with the apple. If you want the apple to be soft and warm, cook it along with the oats.

2 cups apple juice or cider
1 tsp cinnamon
1 apple, cored and chopped

$2 TOTAL
$1 / SERVING

SAVORY OATMEAL: Cook the oatmeal with scallions. Just before it's done, add cheese. Melt the butter in a pan on medium heat. Crack in the eggs, then cover. Fry until the yolks are runny but the whites are cooked, then top each bowl of oats with one fried egg!

2-3 scallions, finely chopped
¼ cup sharp cheddar, grated
1 tsp butter
2 eggs

$1.50 TOTAL
$0.75 / SERVING

Yogurt Smash!

There are so many types of yogurt in the grocery store: some low in fat and high in sugar, some with cute animal pictures. Some are Greek. Some have chocolate shavings and candy. Some have names like "key lime pie."

Now forget about all of that. The best value for your money are the big buckets of plain yogurt. The fat content is your choice—just check that it doesn't contain gelatin and you're all set. Starting with plain yogurt, you can make super flavors in your own kitchen, where you know exactly what's going into it.

If you have kids, ask them what flavors they can imagine and go make it! It's a lot more fun than letting the supermarket choose for you. Try something new and smash it in! Check out the ideas on the adjoining page.

If you want a thicker Greek-style yogurt, all you have to do is strain regular American yogurt through cheesecloth to remove the extra water.

Yogurt's versatility makes it a great staple to keep in the fridge. Mix it with some of the items you see on the next page or turn it into a savory sauce like raita (p. 164) or tzatziki (p. 165).

jam!

yogurt

honey!　coconut!　raspberry!

Soup

It's a cliché, but as soon as the weather gets cold, my apartment fills with the smell of vegetables simmering for soup. Vegetable soups are so simple that you can easily invent your own, using the stuff you and your family like. Start with some onion, carrot, celery, maybe a pepper; then add broth and a large amount of, say, spinach, and suddenly you have spinach soup! It's a great way for new cooks to gain some confidence. Just remember to season it enough. Dunk a grilled-cheese sandwich in it and even mediocre soup tastes great.

This thick lentil soup is a flavor-packed staple of the Indian table. There are a ton of ways to prepare dal, but the core—beyond the lentils themselves—is usually ginger, garlic, and chili, along with some dry spices.

Dal

$2.40 TOTAL
$0.60 / SERVING

2 cups lentils
1 tbsp butter
1 onion, finely chopped
1 tsp cumin seeds
1 tsp black mustard seeds
1 tsp turmeric powder
2 cloves garlic, finely chopped
1 green chili, finely chopped
½ inch ginger root, grated
  salt and pepper

You can use any type of lentil you like. If you're using larger lentils (like chana dal, french lentils, or split mung beans), soak them for 30 minutes to start. If you're using the small orange lentils, then don't bother soaking them; they cook very quickly.

Melt butter in a saucepan on medium heat. Add the onion and let it cook for 1 minute, then add the cumin and mustard seeds and stir them around with the onions until they sizzle. Toss in the turmeric powder, garlic, and chili and cook for 3 to 4 more minutes. Add the ginger root and stir fry quickly for about 30 seconds.

Add the lentils along with enough water to cover them, then place a lid on top. Let everything cook for 20 to 45 minutes, or until the lentils are tender. Taste the dal and add salt and pepper. You'll probably need a fair bit of salt to bring out all the flavors—a teaspoon or so.

If you have them available, top the dish with a splash of cream or some chopped fresh cilantro.

Corn Soup

FOR FOUR TO SIX

This thick, sweet, satisfying soup is a favorite of kids and adults. This is wonderful to make at the beginning of autumn when corn on the cob is at its peak, but canned corn can also make it a warm reminder of summer in the depths of winter.

4 cups corn, fresh, canned, or frozen
1 tbsp butter
1 onion, finely chopped
2 sticks celery, finely chopped
1 green or red bell pepper, finely chopped
1 small potato, diced
4 cloves garlic, finely chopped
1 chili pepper, finely chopped (optional)
1 tbsp cornmeal or flour
  salt and pepper

CORN BROTH
4 to 8 cobs corn, with corn removed
2 bay leaves (optional)
  salt

ALTERNATE BROTH
5 cups vegetable broth or chicken stock

If you're making this soup with corn on the cob, the first step is to make corn broth. If you're using canned or frozen corn, you'll also need chicken or vegetable broth instead. In that case, skip the next paragraph.

To make corn broth, place the cobs and bay leaves in a large stockpot and cover with water. Bring to a boil over high heat, then turn the heat down to medium and let the water boil for about 30 minutes. Taste the broth and add salt and pepper until it tastes lightly corny. Boil it down until you have about 5 cups of liquid. The broth will keep for several months if frozen, or a few weeks in the refrigerator.

To make the soup, melt the butter in a large pot or Dutch oven on medium heat. Add onion, celery, bell pepper, and potato, then stir. Cover the pot and let everything fry and steam for about 5 minutes.

Take the lid off the pot and add the garlic and chili pepper, if using. Stir the vegetables, using a splash of water or broth to free any that get stuck to the bottom of the pot.

Let the vegetables cook, stirring occasionally, for another 5 minutes. They should be lightly browned and soft, although the potatoes will not be fully cooked yet.

Add the corn and cornmeal or flour to the pot and stir. Cover with about 5 cups of broth and bring to a boil, then turn the heat down to low and simmer for about 30 minutes. The broth will thicken and become opaque.

Add salt and pepper to taste. If you made your own corn broth, you'll probably need at least a teaspoon of salt; if you used store-bought broth, you'll need less.

Serve with a slice of garlic bread or add a hard-boiled egg for extra protein.

$5 TOTAL
$1.25 / SERVING

$9 TOTAL
$1.50 / SERVING

French Onion Soup

FOR SIX

Best if you accept it now: you are going to cry making this recipe, since the first step is to chop a mountain of onions. But crying is good for us from time to time. Soon you will be on to the magical part, watching a colossal pile of onions shrink and caramelize to make a sweet, flavorful, wonderful soup. Save this recipe for the winter, when other vegetables are out of season and you want to fill your home with warm aromas. As my friend Marilyn, who suggested this recipe, said, "the smell in your kitchen is absolute heaven."

4 lb onions, any type

4 cloves garlic

2 tbsp butter

2 bay leaves

1 tbsp vinegar, any type (optional)

3 tsp salt

  pepper

8 cups water

6 slices bread

1½ cups cheddar, grated

ADDITIONS

beef or chicken stock instead of water

red wine

chili flakes

fresh thyme

Chop each onion in half lengthwise, peel them, then cut them into half-moon slices. These big slices are fine since you're cooking the onions for so long. Slice the garlic as well.

Melt the butter in a large pot on medium heat. Add the onions, garlic, and bay leaves. Cover the pot with a lid and leave it for 10 minutes. When you come back, the onions should have released a lot of moisture. Give them a stir. Pour in the vinegar and put the lid back on.

Cook for 1 hour, stirring every 20 minutes. When the onions at the bottom start to stick and turn dark, add a splash of water to unstick them. Don't worry, the onions aren't burning, just caramelizing. The water helps lift off the sticky, delicious, sweet part!

Once the onions are very dark and about a quarter the volume they once were, add all the water and a bunch of salt and pepper. Cover the pot again, turn the heat down to low, and let it simmer for another hour. Taste and adjust salt and pepper as needed.

Ladle the soup into bowls.

Now it's time to make cheese toast! If you want classic French onion soup—with the toast directly in the soup, which makes it a bit soggy—place a piece of bread on top of each bowl of soup, sprinkle with cheese, then heat the bowls under your oven's broiler until the cheese is bubbly.

If you don't like soggy toast, just make the cheese toast on its own and serve it on the side to dunk.

Lightly Curried Butternut Squash Soup

FOR FOUR

Squash is almost the perfect vegetable for soup: it's flavorful and has a divinely smooth texture when cooked and puréed. Serve this soup to people who think they don't like squash or curry, and you'll change some minds. You can substitute any winter squash for the butternut; I just like butternut because it's faster to peel and chop than its many cousins.

1 butternut squash
  or other winter squash
1 tbsp butter
1 medium onion, diced
1 green bell pepper, diced
3 cloves garlic, finely chopped
1 tsp cumin powder
1 tsp coriander powder
1 tsp turmeric powder
1 tsp cayenne pepper
1 can coconut milk
3 cups water
  salt and pepper

OPTIONAL
sour cream
scallions
fresh cilantro

To prepare the squash, peel off the tough skin with a potato peeler. Cut the squash in half lengthwise with a sharp chef's knife, then scoop out the seeds and gloop. (You can save the seeds for a tasty snack later, if you like: just clean the gloop off, then toast them.)

Next, slice off the stem and very bottom of the squash and throw them away. Take each half of the squash and place it face-down on a cutting board. Chop each into ½" slices, then turn each slice into cubes.

Put a large pot or Dutch oven on the stove on medium heat. Melt the butter and let the pot get hot. Add the onion, pepper, and garlic, then sauté for two minutes.

Add the cubed squash and spices and stir it all together. Put a lid on the pot and let it cook for another two minutes. Add the coconut milk and water and stir.

Bring the soup to a boil, then turn down the heat to low and let it cook for about 30 minutes, or until the squash is tender.

Once the squash is tender, taste the soup and add salt and pepper as needed. Soup usually needs a fair bit of salt, so be generous.

If you have an immersion blender, you can purée the soup in the pot. If you have a normal blender, wait until the soup has cooled before transferring it to the blender. Purée until smooth, then taste again and add any more salt and pepper it might need.

You can enjoy the soup as-is or serve it with another drizzle of coconut milk or a dollop of sour cream, plus some chopped scallions or cilantro.

Salad

There isn't much to a great salad: just
fresh vegetables, anything crunchy, and
one or two rich ingredients like cheese,
nuts, a buttery crouton, or a creamy
dressing. The dressing should be well
seasoned with salt and have a nice hit of
vinegar or citrus to bring out the other
flavors. Don't bother with store-bought
dressing. It usually tastes lousy and is
full of cheap oils and chemicals; you
can make better and cheaper dressing
at home with just a few pantry items.
Salad shouldn't be a side dish you
grudgingly serve as an afterthought.
Make it a meal you look forward to by
building it around your favorite flavors.

Broiled Eggplant Salad

FOR TWO

Even if you aren't a big eggplant fan, you might enjoy this despite yourself. Broiled eggplant has a crunchy and meaty texture, and the tahini dressing makes the salad rich and creamy.

1 medium eggplant, sliced into circles
1 tbsp lemon juice
1 tbsp tahini
　sprinkle of chili flakes (optional)
　fresh dill, finely chopped (optional)
　salt and pepper

Turn on your oven's broiler. Arrange the slices of eggplant on a baking sheet, then place them under the broiler for about 3 minutes. Watch them carefully. Once they begin to blacken, remove them from the oven and flip the slices over. Repeat the process on the other side. Once your eggplant is nicely charred, chop it into bite-sized pieces.

In a bowl, mix the tahini, lemon juice, and chili flakes (if using), plus plenty of salt and pepper. Add the eggplant and stir it around. Add more salt or lemon juice according to your taste, then top it with dill if available, and serve!

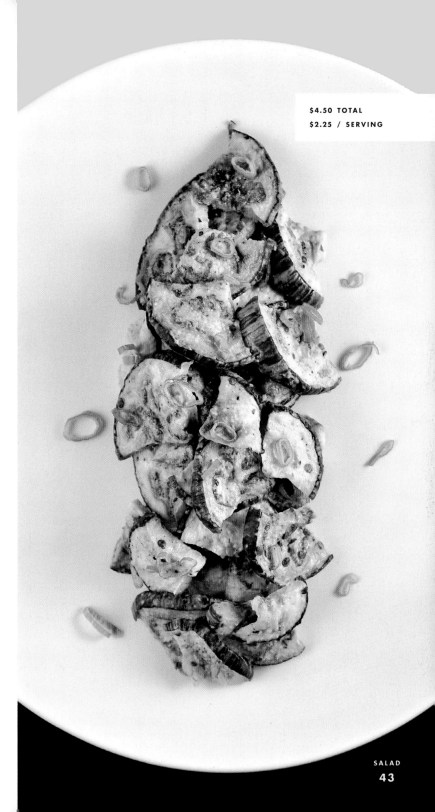

$4.50 TOTAL
$2.25 / SERVING

Kale Salad

FOR TWO, OR FOUR AS A SIDE

This kale is treated
like romaine lettuce
in a Caesar salad. The
bitterness of the greens
is delicious alongside
the rich, fatty dressing.
You could also use
Swiss chard. If you're
worried about the
raw egg yolk in the
dressing, feel free to
omit it.

1 large bunch kale

2 cups bread cubes

2 tbsp butter (more as needed)

salt and pepper

Romano or Parmesan,
freshly grated

DRESSING

1 egg yolk, raw, from a
high-quality fresh egg

2 tsp lemon juice

2 tsp Dijon mustard

1 clove garlic, finely grated
(optional)

1 anchovy, finely chopped
(optional)

3 tbsp olive oil

salt and pepper

Start by making croutons (p. 146).

To make the dressing, drop the egg yolk into a large mixing bowl. Add the lemon juice, mustard, garlic, and anchovy. Whisk briskly until the dressing is light and frothy. Slowly add the olive oil, whisking the whole time. Once everything is incorporated, add the salt and pepper, then adjust to your taste. I like it very lemony.

Cut the kale leaves to remove the large stem from the center. (Lacinato kale, sometimes called Tuscan kale, has the easiest stems to remove.) Slice the leaves in half lengthwise, then cut into thin ribbons. Chopping the kale into small pieces disguises its tough texture.

Toss the kale in the bowl to coat it with dressing. Set aside for 10 minutes or leave in the fridge for a few hours. The kale will become tender as it marinates.

Before serving, toss in the croutons and top with Romano cheese.

$4.50 TOTAL
$2.25 / SERVING

Smaller potatoes are best, but whatever you've got will be fine! If you're using very large potatoes, chop them into halves or quarters to speed up the cooking—or dice them into bite-sized pieces if you're really in a hurry. Otherwise, keep the potatoes whole.

Cover the potatoes with water in a large pot with a lid. Bring the water to a boil over medium-high heat, then turn the heat down to medium and set the lid askew so that steam can escape.

After about 25 minutes, try piercing the largest potato with a fork. If the fork pierces the potato easily, it's fully cooked. If not, boil for 5 more minutes. It's fine if they're a little overcooked, but undercooked potatoes are awful.

Drain the water. Once the potatoes are cool enough to handle safely (but still warm), roughly chop them into bite-sized pieces, if you haven't already.

In a large bowl, mix the olive oil, citrus juice or vinegar, mustard, salt, and pepper. Whisk it briskly until the liquid is blended. If you don't have a whisk, simply whip with a fork.

Throw the potatoes into the bowl and stir to coat them in the dressing. Add a generous amount of salt as you stir. Potatoes are very bland without salt! Then let them marinate for 10 minutes.

Chop a handful of scallions and sprinkle them over top. Toss the salad once more, then taste and adjust the salt, pepper, and vinegar as you see fit.

This keeps very well and travels nicely to a picnic or potluck. Have fun!

Ever-Popular Potato Salad

FOR FOUR

I developed this salad because I'm not a big fan of mayonnaise-based potato salads. This is really the simplest thing: just potatoes in a regular vinaigrette. You can add all kinds of extras to it to make it more festive, but people always rave about the salad as is. The secret is that potatoes actually have really nice flavor—all you have to do is season them properly. Let potatoes be potatoes, no need to hide 'em!

If you have leftover roasted potatoes or other root vegetables, the same idea works great. Just skip the cooking part and go straight to the dressing.

2 lb potatoes
2 tbsp olive oil
2 tbsp lemon juice, lime juice, or vinegar
2 tsp Dijon mustard
  salt and pepper
  scallions

ADDITIONS
fresh dill, chopped
fresh parsley, chopped
paprika
fresh chillies, finely chopped
pickles, finely chopped

$3.00 TOTAL
$0.75 / SERVING

$5.20 TOTAL
$1.30 / SERVING

Spicy Panzanella

FOR FOUR

A former classmate, George, likes salads with a little kick. (As you can maybe tell, I do too!) For inspiration, I turned to panzanella, a classic Italian bread-and-tomato salad. The Italians are true masters of making leftovers delicious. Here, old hard bread soaks up tomato juice and dressing for a super flavorful and filling salad. You can toss in any vegetable or fruit so long as it's juicy. Bell peppers or carrots won't work so well, but peaches, grapes, and zucchini all do. If you don't like spicy salads as much as George and I do, feel free to replace the jalapeño with garlic or shallot.

2 small field cucumbers
  or 1 English cucumber, chopped
2 medium tomatoes, chopped
  salt and pepper
4 slices day-old bread

DRESSING

1 jalapeño, finely chopped
2 tbsp tomato, chopped
1 lime, juiced
2 tbsp olive oil
  salt and pepper

ADDITIONS

fresh herbs
peaches, nectarines, or plums
red onion, finely chopped
zucchini or summer squash
olives
grapes

If you're using field cucumbers—usually much less expensive than English cucumbers—peel them roughly to remove the tough skin.

Keep about 2 tablespoons of chopped tomatoes aside to use in the dressing, but throw the rest of the tomatoes and all the cucumbers into a large bowl. Sprinkle generously with salt and pepper; the salt helps draw out the juices. Toss the vegetables quickly.

Place a small saucepan on medium heat with a few drops of olive oil. Sauté the jalapeño for about a minute, then add the remaining tomato and a tablespoon of water. Cook for another 2 minutes, until the tomato juices release. Sprinkle liberally with salt and pepper.

Once the water has evaporated, turn off the stovetop and dump the jalapeño-tomato mixture on your cutting board. Chop it very finely, then throw it back into the pan—with no heat—along with the lime juice and olive oil. Taste it and add more salt and pepper as needed. You've got dressing!

Chop or tear the bread into bite-sized pieces, then toast it in a skillet over medium heat, tossing occasionally until the bread chunks are toasty on all sides. Alternatively, just toast full slices of bread in a toaster and tear them up afterwards, or skip the toasting entirely if the bread is already super-hard.

Mix the bread and vegetables with the dressing. Taste and adjust salt and pepper once more.

Let it sit for a few minutes so that the bread can soak up the juices, then serve!

Cold (and Spicy?) Asian Noodles

FOR FOUR

On a hot day, this is all I want to eat. Cold but spicy food is refreshing and delicious in the summer. If you have some spice oil on hand, be sure to add it. It's amazing in this.

12 oz dried spaghetti, soba, or any Asian noodles
2 tbsp soy sauce
1 bunch scallions, chopped
1 cucumber, finely chopped
salt and pepper

ADDITIONS
spice oil (p. 162)
peanut sauce (p. 161)
grated carrot
shredded cabbage
bean sprouts
hard-boiled egg
chopped tomato

Prepare the noodles according to the package instructions. Rinse them under cold water and put them in a colander to drain.

Put the noodles in a bowl and add the soy sauce, spice oil if you have it, scallions, and cucumber (and any other additions). Mix it all together with a fork or a tongs. Taste it and add salt and pepper or more spice oil as needed.

Let the noodles sit in the fridge for about an hour if you can. The flavors will mingle and become more intense.

Think of this as a recipe that you can really make your own. Use whatever sauce or dressing you like and whatever vegetables you have around, or just a few scallions.

$5 TOTAL
$1.25 / SERVING

Taco Salad

FOR TWO

This salad is a great use for leftover beans (or pulled pork)—crunchy, fresh, yet satisfying enough to be a whole meal. I like to make taco salad in a week where I've made a large batch of beans and I'm craving something fresh.

4 cups lettuce, chopped
1 cup beans, pulled pork, or ground beef
2 small tomatoes, chopped
½ cup corn, canned or fresh
2-3 scallions, finely chopped
1 cup tortilla chips, roughly crushed
sharp cheddar or queso fresco, for sprinkling

DRESSING
¼ cup sour cream or yogurt
juice of one lime
salt and pepper

ADDITIONS
cucumber
jalapeño
bell peppers
grated carrots
salsa (p. 163)

Mix up the dressing and taste it. Adjust the salt, pepper, and lime to your liking.

Mix the other ingredients in a large bowl. Pour the dressing over just before serving and toss to coat the salad evenly. Eat immediately, maybe with a few extra tortilla chips on the side.

$5.20 TOTAL
$2.60 / SERVING

Beet and Chickpea Salad

FOR TWO

This dish is spicy, crunchy, and almost certainly the pinkest salad you'll ever eat! Don't be scared.

2 to 3 beets, peeled and grated
1 cup chickpeas, cooked or canned
3 tbsp peanuts

DRESSING
1 tbsp lime juice
1 tsp chili sauce
1 tbsp olive oil
  salt and pepper

Peel the raw beets, removing the stems if necessary, then shred the beets with a box grater. Place the beets in a bowl along with the chickpeas and nuts.

Mix up the dressing ingredients in another small bowl and stir to combine. Taste and adjust the salt and pepper to your liking.

Add the dressing to the other bowl and mix up all the ingredients. Let it sit for about 5 minutes so that the flavors can soak into the vegetables and the beet juices can mingle with the dressing.

$3.50 TOTAL
$1.75 / SERVING

$3.20 TOTAL
$0.80 / SERVING

Broccoli Apple Salad

FOR FOUR

The bitterness of broccoli is delicious next to the sweet tartness of apples. Plenty of crunch, too!

1 large crown and stem of broccoli

2 apples

DRESSING

1 lemon, juiced

1 tbsp olive oil

salt and pepper

ALTERNATE DRESSING

1 tbsp yogurt

1 tsp olive oil

1 tsp lemon juice

1 tsp fresh dill, chopped

salt and pepper

Slice the stem of the broccoli into ⅛" discs. If you can't get them that thin, don't worry, but the thinner the better if you have the patience! Once you reach the crown of the broccoli, cut each of the florets off and slice each of them as thinly as you can as well. Set the broccoli in a bowl.

Halve and core the apples, then place the apples flat side down on your cutting board to make them easier to slice. Slice the apples into ⅛" pieces as well, then dump them into the same bowl.

Choose either of the dressing options and prepare it by simply mixing the ingredients together in a small bowl. Taste it and season with more salt and pepper to match your preferences.

Pour the dressing over the bowl of vegetables and mix it all together.

If you put a plate in the fridge for 10 minutes before serving the salad, it'll stay crisp slightly longer. For the best presentation, pile the salad as high and tight as you can manage.

Charred Summer Salad

FOR TWO, OR FOUR AS A SIDE

$5.50 TOTAL
$2.75 / SERVING

One of the early supporters of this book, Gina, can't eat gluten and wanted more Mexican-inspired options. I designed this spicy summer salad for her, topped with popcorn for a crunch like croutons. Use smaller zucchini, and save the big ones for muffins (p. 21). If you own a grill, use it instead of the broiler!

2 medium zucchini
2 cobs corn
1 tbsp olive oil or vegetable oil
  salt and pepper
2 oz cotija or feta, crumbled
1 cup popcorn (p. 74), popped

DRESSING
1 lime, juiced
1 tbsp olive oil
½ tsp chili powder
  salt and pepper

Chop off both ends of the zucchini, then slice each into four long sticks. Shuck the corn. Lay the zucchini and corn on a baking tray, then rub them with oil, making sure they're well coated. Sprinkle with salt and pepper.

Broil (or barbecue) for 2 to 5 minutes, depending on how powerful your broiler is. Turn the corn over to make sure it cooks evenly. The zucchini should start to blacken in some spots. This is good! Broil for another 2 to 5 minutes, until the vegetables are lightly charred.

Mix the dressing in a large bowl. Taste it and adjust.

Chop the zucchini into bite-sized pieces and slice the corn kernels from the cob. Transfer the vegetables into the bowl with the dressing. Add the crumbled cotija or feta and mix. Sprinkle popcorn (p. 74) over top, then dust with a little extra chili powder, salt, and pepper.

Snacks, Sides & Small Bites

When cooking on a budget, snacks are often the first thing you shave away. If you're creative, though, you can make plenty of cheap, healthy and delightful snacks to enjoy in all seasons and on any occasion. (And remember, leftovers make great snacks, too!)

Jacket Sweet Potatoes

FOR FOUR

$4.80 TOTAL
$1.20 / SERVING

I like to serve these with all kinds of toppings, usually leftovers from other meals. Try filling them with roast chicken, beans and cheese, corn and tomatoes—whatever you have around.

4 large sweet potatoes
  salt and pepper
¼ cup sour cream
½ bunch scallions, finely chopped

Heat the oven to 400 °F. Scrub the sweet potatoes and stab them with a fork a few times. Lay them on a baking sheet.

Bake for 60 to 75 minutes. Because sweet potatoes vary greatly in size, check them after an hour by stabbing with a long knife. If it goes through easily, they're ready. If not, bake longer.

Let cool for 15 minutes. Make a long cut along the top of each potato and open them gently, beating with a fork to fluff up the soft, orange middle.

Sprinkle with salt and pepper. Let each person add sour cream and scallions (or more salt and pepper) to their taste.

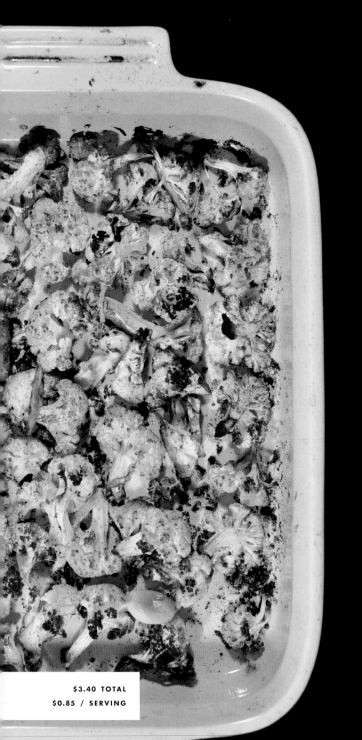

$3.40 TOTAL
$0.85 / SERVING

Smoky and Spicy Roasted Cauliflower

FOR FOUR

Roasted veggies are always delicious, but there's something magical that happens to cauliflower in the oven. It gets so crispy and nutty, and that flavor is brought out even more with the spices here. I'm happy to just eat a bowl of this for dinner, maybe with an egg on top.

1 head cauliflower, cut into small pieces
2 cloves garlic, unpeeled
1 tbsp butter, melted
1 tsp smoked paprika
½ tsp cayenne pepper
salt and pepper

Turn the oven to 400 °F.

In a medium-sized roasting pan, arrange the cauliflower pieces and the unpeeled cloves of garlic. Pour the butter over the cauliflower and then sprinkle the spices over top. Use your hands to thoroughly coat the cauliflower with butter and spices.

Bake for 45 minutes to 1 hour, depending on how crispy you like the florets. Squeeze the roasted garlic throughout and trash the skins.

Spicy Green Beans

FOR TWO

Whenever I make these, I think, "why don't I have this every day?" Throw a fried egg on top, serve with rice, and you have a delicious meal.

1 tsp vegetable oil
½ lb green beans, ends trimmed, chopped into bite-size pieces
2 cloves garlic, finely chopped
1 tsp soy sauce
1 tsp sambal oelek (or 2 tsp chili flakes)

ADDITIONS
1 tsp ginger, grated
1 tsp lemon juice

Add the vegetable oil to a frying pan on medium heat. Once it's hot, add the green beans. Let them cook undisturbed for about 1 minute.

Mix the garlic, soy sauce, and sambal oelek in a bowl (and the ginger and lemon juice, if using).

The beans should have turned bright green. Add about ¼ cup of water to the pan. Cook another 2 minutes, until the water is mostly gone. Pour the sauce into the pan and toss gently to coat. Cook another 2 minutes, until everything is fragrant and most of the liquid is gone. Poke the beans with a fork: if it goes through easily, they're done. They should take about 5 minutes.

Taste and add more chili sauce or soy sauce if you want the beans hotter or saltier.

$1.30 TOTAL
$0.65 / SERVING

$4 TOTAL
$1 / SERVING

Mexican Street Corn

FOR FOUR

This recipe takes fresh, sweet summer corn—already amazing—and adds salt, tang, and spice to the experience. If you have an outdoor grill, prepare the corn that way, but for those without, a broiler is a great shortcut!

4 cobs corn

4 tbsp mayonnaise

½ cup cotija, queso blanco, feta, Romano or Parmesan, grated

chili powder

1 lime, sliced into wedges

Turn your oven's broiler up to high.

Peel off the outer layers of the corn and clean off all the corn silk. Leave the green ends attached for a convenient handhold.

Place the cobs on a baking pan under the broiler for 2 to 3 minutes, then rotate them and repeat until they're brown and toasty all the way around. The broiling shouldn't take more than 10 minutes total.

Working quickly, spread a tablespoon of mayonnaise over each cob, lightly coating every kernel. Next, sprinkle the cheese all over the corn. It should stick fairly easily to the mayonnaise, but you'll probably get a little messy coating them thoroughly.

Sprinkle chili powder over the corn, but not too heavy or it'll be gritty. Use any chili powder you like; ancho or cayenne are great.

Lastly, squeeze lime juice all over and serve hot!

$3.50 TOTAL
$1.75 / SERVING

Green Chili and Cheddar Quesadillas

FOR TWO

4 tortillas (p. 137)
½ cup sharp cheddar, grated
½ cup green chilies, canned or fresh, chopped
1 tbsp fresh cilantro, chopped

These are a great snack or a quick meal, and you can add pretty much anything to them! To make 'em cheaper, use fresh tortillas (p. 137).

Spread ¼ cup of green chilies evenly over one tortilla. Sprinkle ¼ cup of cheese over the chilies, then top with half the cilantro. Place another tortilla on top of each prepared tortilla to form a quesadilla. Repeat!

Place a large, non-stick pan on medium heat. Once it's hot, add a quesadilla and toast for about 1 minute. Flip it over and brown the second side, then do the same for the other quesadilla. Slice into triangles and enjoy with some fresh salsa (p. 163) and sour cream.

Cornmeal Crusted Veggies

FOR FOUR

These are kind of like having veggie french fries. The cornmeal makes them super crunchy, and they're great with a dipping sauce. Might I suggest peanut sauce (p. 161)? This breading process can be done with almost any vegetable; some of my favorites include zucchini wedges, bell peppers, and cooked winter squash. It's sort of like fried green tomatoes or okra, but this baked version skips the expense and mess of the oil, yet keeps the crunch.

½ lb green beans, stems cut off
½ cup all-purpose flour
2 eggs
¼ cup milk
1 cup cornmeal
1 tsp salt
1 tsp black pepper
1 tsp paprika
½ tsp garlic powder

ALTERNATIVES
zucchini
bell pepper sticks
winter squash
cauliflower florets
broccoli florets
okra
carrot sticks

Heat the oven to 450 °F.

Set up your breading station! On one plate, spread out the flour. Crack both eggs into a bowl, add the milk, and mix lightly with a fork. On another plate, spread the cornmeal, salt, black pepper, paprika, and garlic powder. Mix the plate with your fingers.

Spread a small amount of oil or butter across a baking sheet.

A few at a time, take the green beans and dredge them in the flour. Next, transfer the flour-covered beans to the egg mixture. Cover the beans lightly with egg mixture, being careful to shake off any excess egg. Then transfer to the cornmeal mixture and coat them evenly.

Carefully spread the crusted green beans onto the baking sheet. Repeat until you've done them all. If you run out of any of the three mixtures, just mix up a bit more.

Bake for 10 to 15 minutes, until golden and crispy. Enjoy hot with your favorite dipping sauce!

Pictured are bell peppers and green beans.

$2.60 TOTAL
$0.65 / SERVING

$2.80 TOTAL
$1.40 / SERVING

Brussels Sprout Hash and Eggs

FOR TWO

This is a great light lunch or side dish. The Brussels sprouts get salty and tangy from the olive and lemon, then crispy and caramelized on the bottom. Mix in the little bit of fat from the egg yolk, and *wow* is this delicious.

4 cups Brussels sprouts, finely chopped
  salt and pepper
1 tbsp butter
3 cloves garlic, finely chopped
6 olives, finely chopped
  lemon juice
2 eggs

Chop off the ends of the sprouts. Slice them in half, then finely shred each half. Place the shreds in a bowl and sprinkle with salt and pepper.

Melt the butter in a non-stick pan on medium-high heat. Swirl it around to coat the pan. Add the Brussels sprout shreds and garlic, then leave it to cook for about 1 minute. Mix it up and toss it around. Add the olives and mix again.

Crack the eggs into separate areas of the pan. Sprinkle them with salt and pepper. Pour in 2 tablespoons of water and cover with a lid. Let the eggs steam, undisturbed, for 2 minutes.

Once the whites of the eggs are cooked through, turn off the heat and sprinkle everything with lemon juice.

Poutine

FOR FOUR

Poutine isn't an everyday meal, but it's a favorite. Since I don't like deep-frying at home, I bake the fries; they still get crispy without the fuss of frying.

Montreal-style poutine is made with vegetable gravy, as in this recipe, but you can also make your favorite beef or turkey gravy.

Of course, proper poutine uses cheese curds, and if you can find them do use those, but fresh mozzarella works for me. It has the same spongy quality, just maybe with a little less squeak. This recipe does comes out a little more expensive than you would think because of the fresh mozzarella. If you use less or skip the cheese entirely, you can cut the price in half.

2-3 medium Russet potatoes, sliced into sticks
2 tbsp vegetable oil
salt and pepper
scallions, chopped
6 oz fresh mozzarella, diced

GRAVY
2 tbsp butter
1 shallot or 3 scallions, finely chopped
3 cloves garlic, finely chopped
2 tbsp all-purpose flour
1½ cups vegetable broth
1 tsp soy sauce
½ tsp cayenne pepper
salt and pepper
6 leaves fresh sage, finely chopped (optional)

Set the oven to 400 °F.

Pour 1 tablespoon of vegetable oil onto a baking sheet. Spread the oil around, then spread out the sticks of sliced potato. Pour the rest of the oil over the top and sprinkle generously with salt and pepper. Use your hands to ensure the potatoes are coated with oil, salt, and pepper, and evenly spread across the pan. Place them in the oven and bake for 20 minutes.

Meanwhile, prepare the gravy. Melt the butter in a saucepan on medium heat. Add the shallot and garlic. Let them cook for 2 minutes until translucent, but not brown. Add the flour and quickly stir with a spoon. Add a little broth if gets too clumpy.

Let the mixture cook until it turns light brown. Add the vegetable broth, soy sauce, and cayenne pepper. Bring the gravy to a boil, then turn down the heat and let it cook for about 5 minutes, stirring occasionally. Taste it, adding salt and pepper as needed. Turn down the heat to very low, just enough to keep the gravy warm until the fries come out of the oven.

Dice the mozzarella.

After the fries have baked for 20 minutes, remove them from the oven. Lift them with a spatula and test their tenderness with a fork. If it goes through easily, the fries are ready. If you want them a little more crispy, flip them over and put them back in the over for a few more minutes.

Once they're done, pile one layer of fries onto a plate. Top with cheese and then the hot gravy. Repeat with a second layer before sprinkling with scallions and more freshly ground black pepper.

$7 TOTAL
$1.75 / SERVING

$1.50 TOTAL
$0.75 / SERVING

Things On Toast

4 slices bread
2 tbsp butter
salt and pepper
topping
fried egg (optional)

I love bread, and toast in particular is my comfort food—I crave it when I'm sick or worn down. Here, I would like to suggest that you take some toast and put something tasty on it. That's it!

Certainly toast can feed a crowd, but I like this meal for times when I'm on my own and want a quick meal or snack. It's a great way to use leftovers or turn a side dish into a full meal.

What makes this more like a special dinner than a quick snack is the way you treat the bread—toasting it in the pan like a nice piece of fish.

A pile of sautéed or raw veggies over buttered, toasty bread is the perfect meal for one and a great way to try a new vegetable. I've suggested a few other toast variations on the following pages, but you can use pretty much any veggie dish from this book or invent your own. Add a fried egg on top if you're extra hungry.

Melt ½ tablespoon of butter in a small pan on medium heat. Place the two slices of bread in the pan and let them cook for about 2 minutes, then lift them with a spatula to check whether they're golden brown underneath. When they are, flip 'em over.

Add the rest of the butter to the pan to make sure the second side of the toast becomes just as golden as the first. Sprinkle the top of the bread with salt and pepper. Once the second side is golden, set the bread on a plate to await its topping.

For the toppings, you can go raw or, as I most often do, sauté veggies or beans with flavors like garlic and chilies, olives and and dill, ginger and turmeric, or any other classic combination (p. 166).

Instead of toast, the topping ideas on the next few pages would also be great over rice or any other grain, in a tortilla, tossed with pasta, or even on a pizza. It's up to you!

$2 TOTAL
$1 / SERVING

PEAS AND LEMON: This is like a less-salty, more-rustic version of the British classic mushy peas. Add a bit of olive oil to a pan on medium heat. Drop in the garlic and peas along with 2 tablespoons of water so that the peas can steam a bit. Leave them until they turn bright green. Sprinkle with lemon juice, Romano, salt, and pepper, then remove the peas from the heat and mash with the back of a fork, either in the pan or in a bowl. Pile onto toast and enjoy!

1 tsp olive oil
2 cloves garlic, finely chopped
1 cup peas, fresh or frozen
1 tsp lemon juice
  Romano or Parmesan, freshly grated
  salt and pepper

$5 TOTAL
$2.50 / SERVING

ASIAN GREENS GRA PROW: This works with any Asian green, from bok choy to tatsoi to gai lan. Splash the oil in a pan on medium heat. Sauté the garlic for 2 minutes, then add the ginger, soy sauce, and the stem part of the greens. Cook for 4 to 5 minutes, until almost tender. Add the leafy part of the greens and cook for 2 more minutes. Turn off the heat and mix in the Thai basil. Taste and add salt and pepper, unless the soy sauce is salty enough on its own.

1 bunch Asian greens, stem separated from leaves
1 tsp vegetable oil
2 cloves garlic, finely chopped
1 tsp ginger root, grated
2 tsp soy sauce
1 handful Thai basil
  salt and pepper

CARAMELIZED ONIONS AND CHEDDAR: Melt the butter in a pan on low heat. Add the onions and let them cook slowly, about 20 minutes. As the onions darken, stir them occasionally, adding a bit of water to loosen up the sticky onion bits on the bottom and keep them from burning. Leave the onions until they're dark purple. They will now be sweet and caramelized. Spread them over toast and top with slices of aged cheddar, salt, and pepper. Put the toast back in the pan and cover with a lid until the cheese is bubbly, then serve it up.

1 tbsp butter
1 red onion, thinly sliced
   sharp cheddar, thinly sliced
   salt and pepper

$2 TOTAL
$1 / SERVING

ROASTED VEGETABLES: This is one of my favorite ways to eat leftover roasted vegetables. Simply create a ridiculously tall pile of vegetables like the winter squash and leeks pictured here, then sprinkle with grated Romano or Parmesan and fresh pepper. You can also add any sauce you have on hand or sprinkle crushed nuts on top.

roasted vegetables (p. 122)
Romano or Parmesan, freshly grated
pepper

$2 TOTAL
$1 / SERVING

$3 TOTAL
$1.50 / SERVING

SALTY BROCCOLI: Warm up the oil in a pan on medium heat. Add the garlic and chili flakes and cook for 2 minutes, until they smell great but are not yet brown. Add the anchovy and cook for another minute. Add the broccoli and about ¼ cup of water. Cover the pan, steam for 3 minutes, then toss and cook for 2 minutes, until the broccoli is tender and the water is gone. Spoon onto toast; top with cheese, salt, and pepper!

1 tsp olive oil
3 cloves garlic, finely chopped
1 tsp chili flakes
1 anchovy, finely chopped
1 crown and stem of broccoli, chopped
    Romano or Parmesan, freshly grated
    salt and pepper

$3.50 TOTAL
$1.75 / SERVING

BROILED EGGPLANT SALAD: Here's yet another use for leftovers—or just a way to make a great salad more substantial. Simply dollop the broiled eggplant salad onto toast, then add some herbs or greens to the top for a fresh counterpoint, along with a bit of cheese.

broiled eggplant salad (p. 43)
fresh herbs or greens
any cheese, crumbled or grated

BLACK-EYED PEAS AND COLLARDS: Oh man, is there anything more comforting than beans on toast? Friends and family will be delighted even if you're secretly using up leftovers. To make the meal a little more fancy, use jalapeño–cheddar scones instead of toast.

black-eyed peas and collards (p. 94)
jalapeño-cheddar scones (p. 22) (optional)

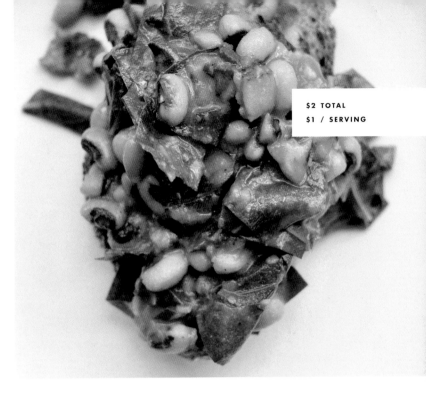

$2 TOTAL
$1 / SERVING

SPINACH AND CHICKPEA: This is a popular tapas dish in Spain. The recipe makes a little more topping than you need for two pieces of toast—but hey, leftovers are tasty. Melt the butter in a pan on medium heat. Add the garlic and cook for 2 minutes. Add the chickpeas and spinach, then cook for 2 to 5 minutes, until the spinach cooks down but is still bright green. Taste and add salt and pepper, then spoon it over toast. If you have it, sprinkle with smoked paprika.

1 tsp butter
2 cloves garlic, finely chopped
1 cup cooked chickpeas
1 bunch spinach
  salt and pepper
  smoked paprika (optional)

$4.50 TOTAL
$2.25 / SERVING

$1 TOTAL
$0.25 / SERVING

Popcorn!

Popcorn is such a great snack. It's easy to forget how easy and cheap it is to prepare at home. Try some different toppings! I've suggested a few on the opposite page.

⅓ cup popcorn
2 tbsp vegetable oil
2 tbsp butter, melted
salt

Place a large pot with a tight-fitting lid on the stove. Pour in the vegetable oil, then the popcorn kernels. Put the lid on and turn the heat to medium.

Using pot holders or oven mitts, occasionally shake the pot from side to side to make sure the kernels are evenly distributed in the oil. Once the popcorn begins to pop, turn the heat down to medium-low and gently shake again.

Once the popping slows down to 5 to 10 seconds between pops, turn the heat off. Wait until you're sure the corn has stopped popping and remove the lid.

Move the popcorn to a bowl and pour butter, salt, and other spices or toppings over top. Gently toss to coat it evenly.

This recipe makes about 10 to 12 cups of popped popcorn—enough for four people. Eat it while it's hot!

SCALLION AND CILANTRO

TURMERIC AND CORIANDER

SPICE OIL (P. 162)

PARM AND BLACK PEPPER

**CAYENNE AND
SMOKED PAPRIKA**

**BROWN SUGAR
AND ORANGE ZEST**

CHILI POWDER AND LIME

PARM AND OREGANO

Handheld

Sometimes you just don't want to deal
with plates and cutlery. Plus, eating
with your hands is fun! These recipes
are great for lunch, dinner, or for a
casual party.

Cauliflower Tacos

FOR TWO TO THREE

This is one of my favorite ways to use roasted cauliflower other than eating it straight. It's a delicious change from the usual vegetable taco offerings. Just look at all those crunchy bits!

roasted cauliflower (p. 58)
6 tortillas
½ cup cheese, grated
½ cup salsa (p. 163) or sauce of choice

Warm up the tortillas in the microwave for 20 to 30 seconds, or put them in a warm oven covered with a towel while you prepare everything else.

Place two to three tortillas on each plate and fill with a generous serving of cauliflower.

Sprinkle the grated cheese over top and drizzle with salsa or sauce of your choice. Enjoy!

$6 TOTAL
$2 - $3 / SERVING

$9 TOTAL
$2.25 / PIZZA

Potato Leek Pizza

MAKES FOUR PIZZAS

Obviously you should just make all kinds of pizza. Seriously, do it. Make it a Thursday-night tradition and an excuse to use up leftovers. *This* pizza, for one, is a fun variation that confounds expectations—proof that, indeed, anything is good on pizza!

pizza dough (p. 139)

2 tbsp olive oil

1 Russet potato or 3 small potatoes, sliced into thin circles

3 leeks, sliced into circles

salt and pepper

1 lb fresh mozzarella, shredded

Turn the oven to 500 °F.

Put a large pan on medium heat and add 1 tablespoon of olive oil. Once the oil is hot, add the potato slices evenly to the pan, making sure each slice is touching the bottom. (If you slice them thin enough, they'll turn out almost like little chips.)

Let them cook until they start to crinkle around the edges and turn brown. Flip them over and brown the other side, then move them to a bowl. Sprinkle with salt and pepper, then toss with your hands (after they cool down!) to make sure they're evenly coated.

Heat up another tablespoon of oil in the same pan, then toss in the leek slices, stirring occasionally until they're soft, about 5 minutes. Toss them with the potato slices and add a bit more salt and pepper.

Clear a space on the counter and sprinkle with flour. Divide your dough into 4 equal pieces. One at a time, stretch the doughs into crusts. You can use a rolling pin or just slowly use your fingers and hands. I like to make mine really thin and big, but it's up to you how thick to make it.

Once the crust is the desired shape and thickness, dust the back of a cookie sheet with flour or cornmeal to keep the crust from sticking, then place it the dough on the sheet.

Now layer it with ¼ of the potato and leek mixture and ¼ of the shredded mozzarella. Bake for 5 to 8 minutes. If it's your first time, simply keep an eye on the oven to see when the pizza's done. The crust should be light brown and the cheese melted.

Repeat the process until you've baked all your pizzas. If your oven is big enough, you can of course do more than one pizza at a time.

Broccoli Rabe and Mozzarella Calzones

MAKES FOUR CALZONES

Calzones are pizza in a slightly different form—a form that lets you stuff in more filling without weighing down the crust. Broccoli rabe is great, but you can use any bitter green, or even broccoli or cauliflower. You'll love these crusty pockets full of oozy goodness!

pizza dough (p. 139)
1 tbsp olive oil
1 large bunch broccoli rabe, chopped
4 cloves garlic, finely chopped
1 tsp chili flakes
2 anchovies, finely chopped (optional)
   salt and pepper
2 cups grated mozzarella cheese

Turn the oven to 500 °F (or as hot as your oven gets). Sprinkle a small amount of flour or cornmeal over a baking sheet and set aside.

Place a large pan on medium heat and add the olive oil. Once the oil is hot, add the tough stem ends of the broccoli rabe and cook for 2 minutes. Next, add the rest of the broccoli rabe, including the leafy parts, along with the garlic, chili flakes, and anchovies. Give the ingredients a stir and let it cook for about 5 minutes, stirring occasionally. Add salt and pepper to taste. The broccoli rabe is done when the stems are tender. Set the filling aside.

Divide the pizza dough into 4 equal pieces. Sprinkle flour over the countertop and place one of the four pieces of dough on it. Using your hands or a rolling pin, roll out the dough as you would for pizza (p. 79).

Roll the dough out quite thin. Pile ¼ of your broccoli rabe mixture and ½ cup of mozzarella onto one side of the circle, leaving a lip around the edge.

Gather up the half of the dough that isn't weighed down with filling and fold it over top. Pinch the edges of the dough together to create a half-moon shape. Place it carefully on the prepared baking sheet and repeat until you have four calzones.

Bake for 6 to 8 minutes or until the calzones are golden-brown on the outside. Be careful when you bite into them—they'll be hot!

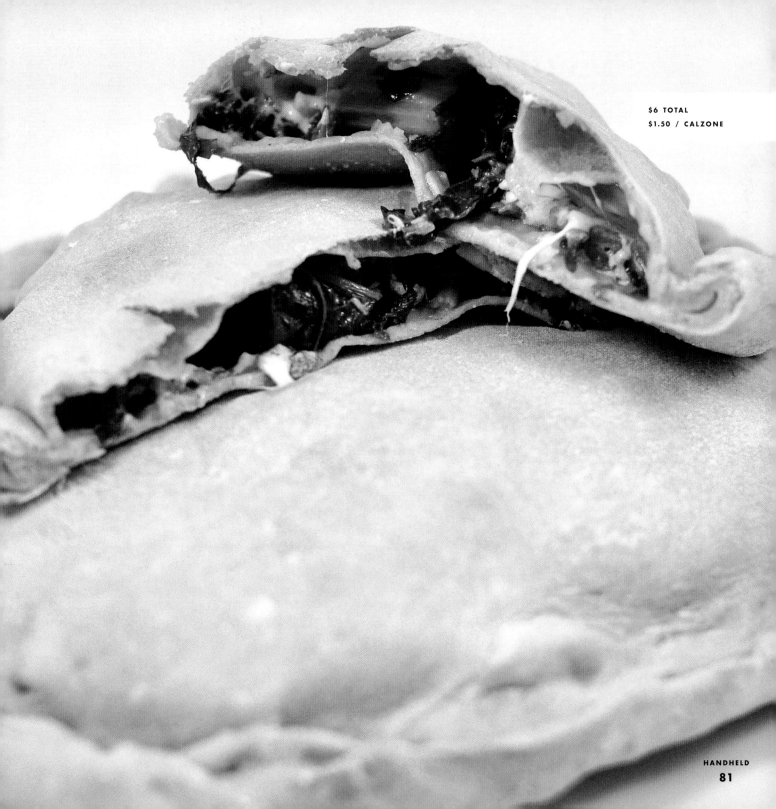

$6 TOTAL
$1.50 / CALZONE

$7.20 TOTAL
$0.60 / EMPANADA

Broccoli, Egg, and Cheddar Empanadas

MAKES TWELVE

In case you can't tell by now, I am partial to tasty dough stuffed with something even tastier. Every culture has its own version, so when you think about it that way, having empanadas, dumplings, perogies, and calzones in one book isn't that crazy—right? My friend Barb felt the same way, so I created this recipe for her.

2 cups all-purpose
   or whole-wheat flour
½ cup cornmeal
½ tsp salt
¼ cup butter
1 egg
½ cup cold water

FILLING
4 cups broccoli with stems,
   chopped
1 cup water
9 eggs
2 cloves garlic, finely chopped
½ tsp chili flakes
   salt and pepper
1 cup sharp cheddar, grated

Mix the flour, cornmeal, and salt in a large bowl. The cornmeal isn't traditional in empanadas—I just like the extra crunch it gives. You can substitute more flour for the cornmeal if you like.

Place the butter in the freezer for 10 minutes, then grate it directly into the flour mixture. Wash and dry your hands, then use them to gently squish the butter into the flour until it looks like bread crumbs.

Make a crater in the flour mixture. Crack the egg into it along with the water. Mix with your hands until it comes together into a smooth ball. If you're using whole-wheat flour and the dough seems dry, add another tablespoon of water. Cover with plastic wrap or a moist towel.

Put the broccoli and water in a pan over medium heat. Cover it with a lid. Cook for 5 to 7 minutes, until the water is gone and the broccoli is tender.

Meanwhile, crack 8 of the eggs into a bowl, saving the last one for an egg wash later. Mix the eggs with the garlic, chili flakes, salt, and pepper.

Once the broccoli is tender, pour the eggs into the pan. Stir until just scrambled, about 2 minutes. Turn off the heat, add the cheese, and stir.

Heat the oven to 400 °F. Lightly oil or butter two baking sheets.

Divide the dough into 12 equal pieces and roll each into a ball. Dust your counter lightly with flour, then use a rolling pin to flatten each ball into a thin circle, a little bigger than a DVD. Place some filling on one side of the circle, then fold over the other side to form a half moon. Pinch the edges and place the empanada on a baking sheet. Repeat!

If you own a pastry brush, an egg wash will make the empanadas shinier. Since it doesn't affect the taste, only how the empanadas look, this step is very optional. In a small bowl, beat an egg with a fork. Brush the tops of the empanadas with the egg wash.

Bake for 20 minutes, until they turn golden brown.

Potato and Kale Rolls with Raita

FOR FOUR

These are a great meal to make when you have leftover roti and raita. The filling comes together in minutes and could be anything, but potatoes and greens are tasty and filling.

8 roti (p. 138)
2 large or 4 medium potatoes, chopped
1 bunch kale or spinach, chopped with stems removed
1 tbsp ghee or butter
1 tsp cumin seeds
½ cup onion, finely chopped
3 cloves garlic, finely chopped
1 tbsp ginger, finely grated
1 tsp turmeric powder
1 tsp coriander powder
1 tsp cayenne powder
  raita (p. 164)
  fresh cilantro

Put a skillet on medium heat and add the ghee or butter. (Ghee, which is traditional in Indian cooking, is just butter with the milk solids removed, and it can withstand higher temperatures than butter without burning.)

Once the butter is hot, add the cumin seeds and let them sizzle for 5 seconds before adding the diced onion. Let the onion cook for 2 minutes, stirring occasionally.

In a small bowl, mix the garlic, ginger, turmeric, coriander, cayenne powder, salt, and 1 tablespoon of water.

Add the spices to the onion mixture and mix, cooking for another 2 minutes. It will smell strongly aromatic. This step is important because the spices become toasted and release their flavor.

Next, add the potatoes. Stir to coat them with the onions and spices. Add about a cup of water and cover the pan with a lid. Let it cook for about 10 minutes, checking occasionally to stir and make sure nothing is burning. Add more water as needed. You want the final mixture to be only a bit moist, but the water helps everything cook evenly.

Test the potatoes with a fork: if you can easily pierce them, they're ready. Once they are, add the kale and stir until the kale is wilted. Taste and add more salt if needed.

To assemble the rolls, scoop ⅛ of the mixture into the center of a roti, distributing it in an even line. Roll it up.

Serve two roti per person with cilantro and a generous dollop of raita, either over the top or on the side.

$5.25 TOTAL
$0.66 / ROLL

Leftovers

Leftovers are convenient, but can seem unappealing, limp, and cold after sitting in the fridge for a couple of days. That's why the sandwich, the wrap, and the taco are your friend. Here are just a few ideas for how to give leftovers a makeover very quickly for a whole new meal!

TOMATO SCRAMBLED EGGS WRAP (P. 15)
Throw the tomato eggs into a wrap and add some roasted potatoes or rice for bulk.

JACKET SWEET POTATOES SPREAD (P. 57)
Mash up leftover baked sweet potatoes, then spread them in a bacon sandwich for a sweet counterpoint.

TOAST TOPPINGS ON ANYTHING (P. 69-73)
Any of the toast toppings would work in a wrap, as a calzone filling, or as a pizza topping.

CAULIFLOWER TACOS (P. 77)
Tacos are the perfect re-use of roasted cauliflower.

CHANA MASALA WRAP (P. 93)
Sounds strange, but spread some herbed mayo on the wrap and then pile in the chana masala.

BLACK-EYED PEAS AND COLLARDS WRAP (P. 94)
Fold the black-eyed peas and collards into a wrap with a little hot sauce or some tzatziki.

VEGETABLE JAMBALAYA BURRITO (P. 97)
Add some salsa or any leftover beans.

CAULIFLOWER CHEESE SANDWICH (P. 113)
Add some crunchy greens and mustard. Yum!

ROASTED VEGETABLES SANDWICH (P. 122)
Add some extra spices or sauces to liven up the vegetables and grill the bread for some crunch.

ROASTED POTATOES AND CHILIES (P. 125)
This dish is great in a taco—just add a little salsa and grated cheese. I like green salsa here.

TILAPIA TACO (P. 126)
For a makeshift fish taco, chop up some crunchy cabbage and cilantro.

Dinner

My favorite meal of the day. For me, eating dinner indicates that the hard work is done: it's time for family, relaxing, and the more optional endeavors. A great dinner is an opportunity to show love to those you are cooking for and to yourself.

$3.50 TOTAL
$1.17 / SERVING

Creamy Zucchini Fettuccine

FOR THREE

Zucchini and summer squash are so abundant in the summer months. This simple pasta is like a lighter, brighter fettuccine alfredo. It also comes together in no time—the veggies will be ready by the time your pasta is cooked. You'll love it, I promise.

½ lb fettuccine
4 tbsp butter
4 cloves garlic, finely chopped
½ tsp chili flakes
2 small zucchini, finely diced
1 lemon, zested

¼ cup cream
½ cup Romano or Parmesan, grated
salt and pepper
fresh basil, finely chopped (optional)

Bring a pot of water to boil over high heat. Salt the water liberally. This is how pasta gets salted, so don't be shy! Most won't end up in the pasta.

Cook the pasta according to the package directions. I prefer my pasta with some bite, so I drain the pasta just before it's finished so it doesn't get mushy when I add it to the vegetable pan to cook slightly more.

Meanwhile, melt a tablespoon of butter in a pan on medium heat. Add the garlic and chili flakes. Let them sizzle for 30 seconds to a minute, then add the zucchini. Stir the vegetables to coat them. Cook for 5 to 7 minutes, stirring occasionally, until some of the water has cooked off and the veggies are tender when stabbed with a fork. Young summer zucchini doesn't need much cooking. Add the lemon zest. Stir!

Drain the cooked fettuccine and add it to the zucchini pan along with the rest of the butter, the cream, and most of the Romano cheese. Toss the fettuccine around the pan to get everything mixed. Add salt to taste and lots of freshly ground pepper. Top with a bit more cheese and serve immediately.

Pasta with Eggplant and Tomato

FOR TWO

This is similar to a traditional pasta alla norma, but without anchovies and ricotta salata. I like to use a tubular pasta for this dish, but you can use anything, even spaghetti. The eggplant and tomatoes come together into a sauce that is thick and jammy and savory.

½ lb pasta (rigatoni or similar)
2 tbsp olive oil
1 large eggplant, cubed
4 cloves garlic, finely chopped
½ tsp chili flakes
2 cups canned tomatoes, finely diced
¼ cup Romano or Parmesan, freshly grated
   salt and pepper
   fresh basil, finely chopped (optional)

Put a pot of water on high heat and add a good shake of salt. Bring it to a boil and cook the pasta according to the package instructions.

While the water is coming to a boil, splash the olive oil into a wide pan on medium-high heat. Let it get hot. Add the eggplant cubes and sprinkle them with salt, then cook for about 5 minutes. If the eggplant starts to look too dry, add a bit of water.

Once the cubes are a little brown on all sides, add the garlic and chili flakes and stir. Add the tomatoes and cook for about 15 minutes, stirring occasionally. Again, if it looks too dry, add a bit of water. Everything will shrink up and become a sort of loose, thick sauce. Add half the cheese and half the basil, if you have it.

Once the pasta is cooked, drain it and add it to the saucepan. Toss everything together, then turn off the heat. Add salt and pepper to taste.

Serve it in bowls sprinkled with more Romano and basil.

$5 TOTAL
$2.50 / SERVING

$3 TOTAL
$1.50 / SERVING

Chana Masala

FOR TWO

This Indian chickpea dish is a staple in my home. If you don't have cooked chickpeas around, you can use canned, but it will cost about $1 more.

½ tbsp ghee or ½ tbsp butter plus a splash of olive oil

1 tsp cumin seeds

½ cup onion, diced

1 tsp garlic, finely chopped

1 tsp ginger root, grated

½ jalapeño, finely diced

3 tsp coriander powder

1 tsp turmeric

¼ tsp cayenne powder

½ tsp garam masala powder

1 tsp smoked paprika

½ tsp salt

1 cup canned tomatoes, puréed

2½ cups cooked chickpeas, drained

½ cup water

GARNISH

fresh cilantro

yogurt

Measure out all the spices except the cumin seeds and put them in a small bowl.

Let the ghee (clarified butter) melt in a small saucepan over medium-low heat. (Ghee is the traditional Indian choice, but you can substitute butter and a splash of olive oil if you can't find ghee.) Once the ghee begins to sizzle, add the cumin seeds and stir for about 5 seconds. Add the onion and sauté for 2 minutes. Add the garlic and cook for 1 minute. Add the ginger and jalapeño and cook for 1 more minute. Add the spices and then the puréed tomatoes. Mix, then put a lid on the pan and let everything cook down for 5 to 10 minutes.

Once the tomato has reduced and the ghee starts to separate from the sauce, add the chickpeas and water. Mix, then bring it to a boil before reducing to a simmer. Cook for 10 minutes, then squish a few chickpeas with a spoon to thicken the sauce. Garnish with yogurt and cilantro. For a full meal, serve over rice or with roti.

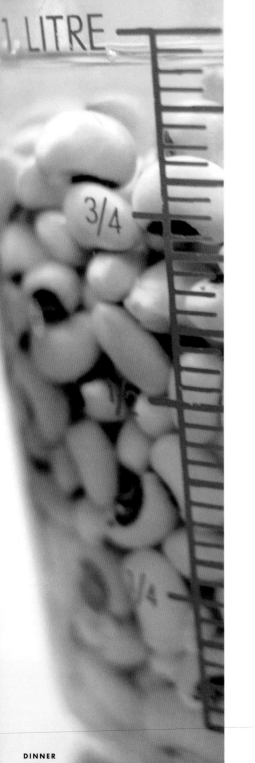

Black-Eyed Peas and Collards

FOR FOUR

This is similar to the southern classic Hoppin' John. If you have them, you can add more vegetables to the base along with the onion—celery, carrot, bell pepper, and some canned tomato would all be great in this. If you want to skip the bacon, just add smoked paprika to replace the smoky flavor.

1 cup dried black-eyed peas	3 strips bacon, cut into small pieces
1 tbsp butter	1 bay leaf
1 large onion, finely chopped	1 large bunch collards
3 cloves garlic, finely chopped	salt and pepper

Soak the black-eyed peas overnight in 4 cups of water.

Melt the butter in a large saucepan on medium heat. Add the onion, garlic, bacon, and bay leaf. Cover the pan with a lid and leave it for 2 minutes. Stir occasionally and cook until the onions are translucent and the bacon is starting to be crispy. Drain the peas and pour them into the saucepan. Cover them with water and turn the heat down to medium-low. Cook for 30 minutes to 2 hours. The cooking time will depend on how old the peas are, which is difficult to predict. The peas are done when you can easily squish them on the countertop with the back of a spoon. Check on them every half hour or so, and if water boils off, add more to cover them.

While the peas cook, line up several collards leaves on your cutting board and slice the tough central stem away from the leaves. Discard the stems. Thoroughly wash the collards, then chop them into bite-sized pieces. Alternatively, use your hands to tear the collards into small pieces.

Once the peas are cooked, add the collards to the pot and put the lid back on. Add 1 teaspoon of salt and some freshly ground pepper, then stir. Taste the liquid and peas and add more salt as needed. Cover the pan with a lid and leave for about 10 to 15 minutes. Once the collards are tender, turn off the heat.

Serve this over rice or any other grain, or with some toast or flatbread.

$5 TOTAL
$1.25 / SERVING

$3.90 TOTAL
$0.65 / SERVING

Vegetable Jambalaya

FOR SIX

I don't make jambalaya exactly the way they do down south, but this vegetable-heavy version is faster and just as good—a great, throw-everything-in-the-pot kind of meal. It's spicy, savory and deeply satisfying. The leftovers are great for making burritos or warmed up with a fried egg on top.

Start with the oil in a large high-sided saucepan over medium-high heat. Add the onion, pepper, and celery, then cook for about 5 minutes, until they become translucent but not brown.

Add the rest of the ingredients except for the rice and broth. Let everything cook for about 1 minute to let some of the tomato juice release.

Add the rice and slowly pour in the broth. Reduce the heat to medium and let the dish cook until the rice absorbs all the liquid. It should take about 20 to 25 minutes.

If you're using any of the additions, throw them in at about the 15-minute mark to let them warm up.

2 tbsp vegetable oil
1 medium onion, chopped
1 green bell pepper, chopped
3 stalks celery, chopped
3 cloves garlic, finely chopped
½ small green chili, finely chopped
2 large tomatoes, chopped
2 bay leaves
1 tsp paprika
1 tsp garlic powder
1 tsp cayenne pepper
½ tsp dried thyme
½ tsp dried oregano
1 tsp salt
1 tsp pepper
1 tsp Worcestershire sauce or soy sauce
¾ cup long grain rice
3 cups vegetable broth or chicken stock

ADDITIONS
slices of fried sausage
shrimp
leftover meat, tofu, or beans

Filipino Chicken Adobo

FOR EIGHT

¾ cup rice vinegar or white vinegar
¼ cup soy sauce
2 cloves garlic, minced
½ tsp black pepper
2 bay leaves
8 chicken thighs, fat trimmed
2 tbsp vegetable oil
¾ cup water
2 medium potatoes, chopped
4 medium carrots, sliced
2 cups white rice
   salt
2 tsp cornstarch

ADDITIONS
4 jalapeños
   ginger root, grated

VARIATIONS
1½ lb pork shoulder or butt, cubed,
   instead of chicken
1 can coconut milk instead of water
   chicken schmaltz instead of vegetable oil

This ultra-adaptable recipe comes to us care of Tony Pangilinan, who grew up on food stamps after his family immigrated from the Philippines "with nothing but four suitcases and a lot of dreams." After several decades of struggling to achieve those dreams, Tony can now help support family members who remain in poverty in the Philippines. Despite their hard circumstances, he notes that his relatives "still feel blessed."

Filipino adobo—very different from Spanish adobo—is basically anything cooked in vinegar, soy sauce, and garlic. Although this version is chicken, you can use any meat or vegetables you like. It's a brilliant dish that turns basic staples into deliciousness. Because it's vinegar-based, it also keeps well in the fridge!

In a large, non-aluminum pan, stir together the vinegar, soy sauce, garlic, pepper, and bay leaves. Add the chicken, coating each piece thoroughly. Cover and let marinate for at least 30 minutes, but overnight is great.

Pull the chicken out of the marinade and pat each piece dry.

Pour the oil into a large pot on medium heat. Once the oil is hot, add enough chicken to fill the bottom of the pot. Let it cook for a few minutes, until one side of the chicken is browned, then flip it over. When the first batch of chicken is done, remove it from the pot and repeat with the remainder.

After all the chicken is browned, put it back in the pot along with the marinade, water, potatoes, and carrots. Turn the heat up until the liquid comes to a boil, then reduce to low heat and simmer for 45 minutes, or until the meat near the bone is no longer pink and the carrots and potatoes are cooked through.

About 20 minutes before the adobo is ready, pour the rice into a medium pot with 4 cups of water. Add two pinches of salt. Bring to a boil over medium heat with the lid off. Turn the heat down and cover with a lid that is slightly askew to let the steam escape. Cook about 20 minutes, until the water is all gone.

Remove the bay leaves from the adobo. In a small bowl, mix the cornstarch with a tablespoon of water, then stir it into the sauce. Let the sauce boil and thicken until the chicken and vegetables are well glazed. Serve over the rice.

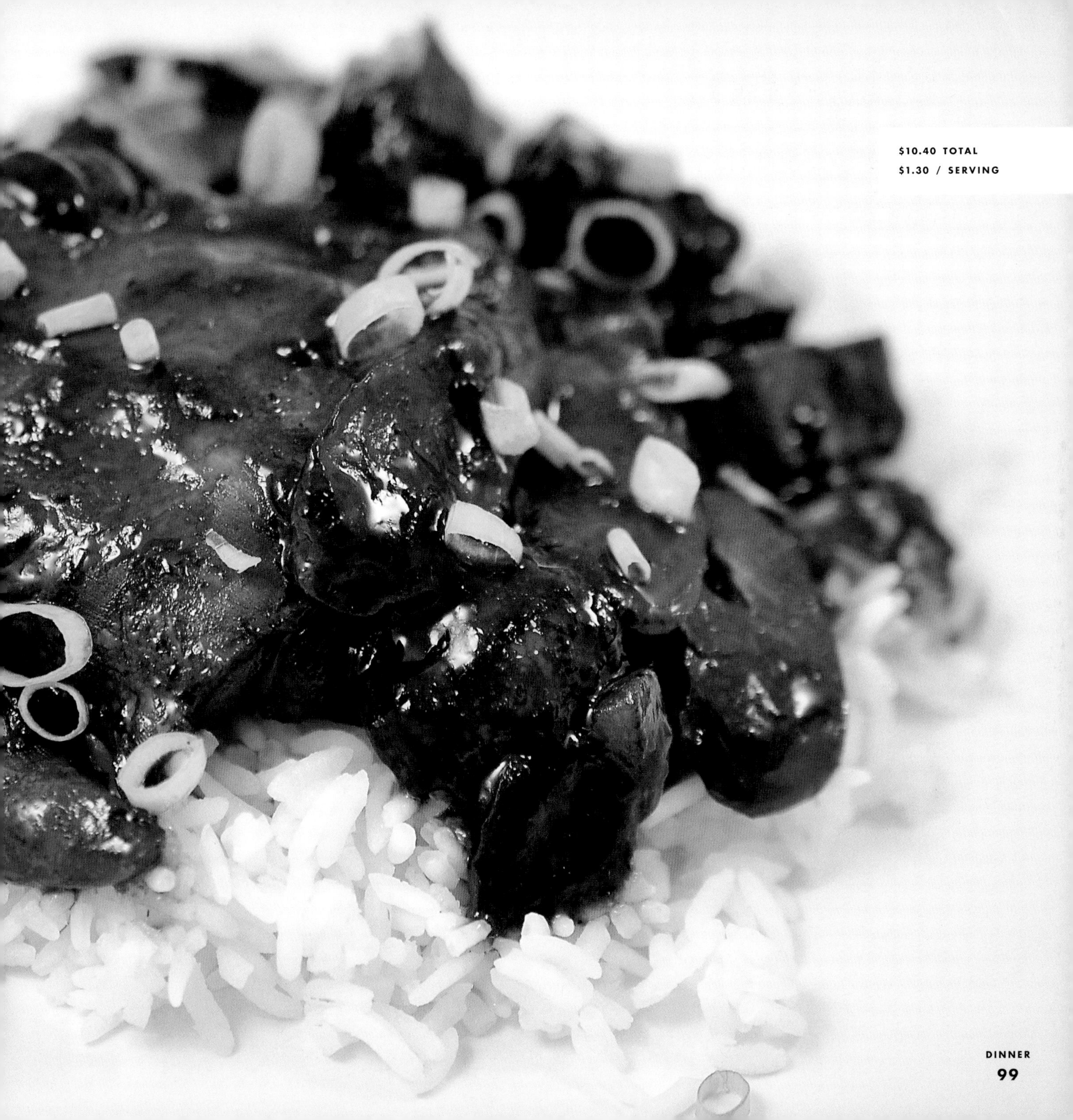

$10.40 TOTAL
$1.30 / SERVING

$3 TOTAL
$1.50 / SERVING

My Dad's Baked Beans

FOR TWO, OR FOUR AS A SIDE

And Mine

FOR TWO, OR FOUR AS A SIDE

My dad loves beans in basically any form. This is his formula for the quickest, easiest way to get beans on his plate without missing out on great flavor. Dad's beans rely on a can of baked beans as the base, while my version uses dried beans you might have left over from another meal. Mine requires a little more cooking and chopping to create the sauce, but comes out even less expensive because of the dried beans. They both taste great, so go with what works best for you: super quick and cheap, or quick and cheaper.

2 cans (27 oz) baked beans

2 tbsp mustard

2 tbsp molasses or brown sugar

2 tsp chipotle en adobo, or any chili sauce

If you're using the chipotle en adobo, chop it finely to be sure the spice will be evenly distributed.

Mix all the ingredients into a pot and heat on the stove until the beans are warmed through. Give it a stir and serve. Or do it all in the microwave—works just as well!

Serve with rice, or just in a bowl. For an English-style breakfast, try spreading the beans over toast. Or throw them into a burrito, or scramble them with eggs, or stir-fry with onions and bell pepper.

3 cups dried pinto, red, or black beans, cooked

½ cup canned tomatoes, puréed or chopped, with juice

¼ onion, finely chopped

2 tbsp mustard

2 tbsp molasses or brown sugar

2 tsp chipotle en adobo, or any chili sauce

VARIATIONS

spicy mustard

no chipotle

TOPPINGS

salsa

scallions

fresh cilantro

avocado

tomato

crumbled bacon

chunks of ham

Cook everything in a pot on medium heat for approximately 5 minutes, or until the juices thicken. That's it!

Half-Veggie Burgers

When a reader named Quinn suggested a recipe that used both lentils and meat, I started thinking about how veggie burgers and beef burgers each have their own strengths. Why not combine the two ideas to create a burger with meaty flavor but the lean protein and low cost of lentils? And so I offer you the half-veggie burger. May it rest a little lighter in your belly.

3 cups lentils or beans, cooked
1 cup bell pepper or other vegetable, finely chopped
1 lb ground beef or other ground meat
1 egg (optional)
 salt and pepper
8 buns

You can use almost any vegetable to make these burger patties, except lettuce and other greens. If you pick a hard vegetable like potato, squash, or eggplant, you'll need to cook it first.

Roughly mash the lentils. Make sure the vegetables are either small to begin with (like corn or peas) or finely chopped so that they cook evenly. I went for a bell pepper this time.

Mix the lentils, veggies, and meat with your hands in a large bowl. If you're going to barbecue, add an egg to keep them from crumbling. Season with salt and pepper. Form into 8 patties.

Grill the patties either on the barbecue or a pan on the stovetop over medium-high heat. Sear until dark brown on one side, then flip 'em and do the same on the other side. If you want cheeseburgers, lay cheese on the patties after flipping them once.

Serve on toasted buns with your favorite condiments and fresh vegetables. Burgers are a great place to be adventurous!

If you won't eat all the burgers at once, wrap the raw patties in plastic. Refrigerate for a few days or freeze for up to 2 weeks.

$7.20 TOTAL
$0.90 / SERVING

$16.50 TOTAL
$2.75 / SERVING

Beef Stroganoff

FOR SIX

Beef stroganoff is one of my husband's favorites, so I make it as a treat for him—and one of my early readers, Dave, says his mother made it for him growing up. It's a classic winter meal from Eastern Europe that warms up a cold house and fills the air with rich aroma. You can use any cut of beef; just adjust the cooking time based on the toughness. Dave's mom made it with red pepper instead of carrot, so feel free to do the same if you can get red peppers at a good price.

1 lb beef chuck or other cut
   salt and pepper
2 tbsp butter
2 onions, chopped
2 large carrots, chopped
1 tbsp flour
2 tsp paprika
4 cups water
3 cloves garlic, finely chopped
1 lb mushrooms, chopped
1 lb egg noodles
½ cup sour cream
3 tbsp mustard

ADDITIONS
½ cup red wine
   potatoes
   fresh dill

Chop the raw beef into bite-sized pieces and season generously with salt and pepper.

Melt half the butter in a large saucepan on medium heat. Toss in enough beef to cover the bottom of the pan. You may need to cook the meat in two batches, depending on the size of your pan. Brown the meat on all sides, then set it aside on a plate.

Add the onions and carrots to the pan and cook until the onions become translucent. Sprinkle with the flour and paprika, then cover with water. Drop the meat back in the pot. Cover the pot with a lid, but leave it askew so the steam can escape. Cook on medium-low heat for 2 hours. This process will make the beef tender and turn the water into beef stock.

If you're using a less tough cut of beef, you don't need to cook nearly as long. Simply brown the meat, then substitute the water for 1 cup of beef stock and cook for 20 minutes. It's a lot quicker, but of course tender meat is more expensive!

Meanwhile, in another pan on medium heat, melt the rest of the butter. Add the garlic and cook for about a minute. Add the mushrooms and toss to coat them with garlic and butter. Sprinkle with salt and pepper. Let the mushrooms cook about 5 minutes, stirring occasionally, until they brown and shrink. Turn off the heat and taste. Add salt and pepper as needed.

Cook the noodles (or any pasta) according to the package instructions. Try to time it to coincide with finishing the stew.

Check on the beef. If the water has reduced to approximately a cup of thick, flavorful liquid and the beef is tender, it's done! If not, let it cook a little longer. Once it's ready, stir in the mushrooms, sour cream, and mustard. Turn the heat down to low to keep it warm until the pasta is ready. Once again, taste and add more salt, pepper, and paprika if needed.

Put the noodles into bowls and top with the stew. Sprinkle a little paprika over top and enjoy!

I got really excited when my friend Iva asked for a recipe that featured the Chinese flavors she grew up with. After all, Chinese cooking depends on the same general principles as *Good and Cheap*: build bright flavors from a few key ingredients; use lots of veggies and just a little meat or fish. The ginger–garlic broth in this hot pot is spectacular! You can use whatever vegetables you have around, but mushrooms help create an earthy broth. The effect of such a small amount of toasted sesame oil is remarkable, too—an investment, but a transformative flavor.

Tofu Hot Pot

FOR FOUR

If you have time, freeze the ginger root for an hour before you start. It's much easier to grate when frozen! Store the rest of the root in the freezer until the next time you need it.

Drop the grated ginger root and garlic into a pot over medium heat. A few seconds later, once you can start to smell the garlic, pour in the water. Bring to a boil, then reduce the heat to low.

Add the mushrooms, chili paste, soy sauce, and toasted sesame oil. Place a lid on the pot and let simmer for 20 minutes.

Separate the white and green parts of the scallions. You'll cook the white and save the green to sprinkle over the soup.

Cut the tofu into four slices, then turn each slice into eight squares. Or just chop it up however you like.

Add the tofu, carrots, and the white parts of the scallions to the broth. Cook about 10 minutes more, until the carrots are tender.

Add the noodles and keep boiling until they soften, usually just a few minutes, although it depends on the type of noodles.

Taste the broth. If it isn't salty enough, splash in more soy sauce. Adjust the sesame oil and chili paste to your taste as well.

Ladle the soup into bowls. For a little crunch, top with bean sprouts and the green bits of the scallions.

If you have leftovers, you'll find you like this soup even more the next day. Overnight, the flavors will infuse into the tofu, as well as combining with each other. You might want to store the noodles separately, though, because otherwise they'll get soggy.

1 tbsp ginger root, finely grated
4 cloves garlic, finely grated
8 cups water
½ lb mushrooms, chopped
1 tsp chili paste
2 tbsp soy sauce
2 tsp toasted sesame oil
4 scallions, chopped
16 oz firm tofu
4 medium carrots, chopped
8 oz dried spaghetti, soba, or any Asian noodles
bean sprouts (optional)

ADDITIONS
chicken, pork, or beef
peanuts, chopped
cabbage, chopped
kimchi
chili peppers
fresh cilantro
daikon radish, sliced

$7.20 TOTAL
$1.80 / SERVING

$9.00 TOTAL
$1.50 / SERVING

Casseroles are a great way to stretch your cooking-without-a-recipe muscles. As one reader, Carolie, reminded me, they require little prep time, yield many meals, and the leftovers are easy to store. Casseroles also let you easily tailor an existing recipe to your own tastes.

So here's my adaptation of one of Carolie's favorite casseroles, itself a play on cabbage rolls, a traditional Eastern European dish that is delicious but labor-intensive. This version is a good way to use up leftover rice or grains and lentils, including leftover rainbow rice (p. 144).

1 tbsp butter

1 fresh sausage, casing removed

1 onion, chopped

4 cloves garlic, finely chopped

1 small or ½ large cabbage, cored and chopped

3 cups cooked rice (p. 144)

4 cups cooked lentils

3½ cups canned tomatoes, puréed, or tomato sauce (p. 142)

salt and pepper

ADDITIONS

breadcrumbs (p. 146) on top

olives

peas or corn

cheese

any spice combination (p. 166)

VARIATIONS

ground beef, turkey, or pork instead of lentils and sausage

swiss chard or collards instead of cabbage

Deconstructed Cabbage Rolls

FOR SIX

Heat the oven to 350 °F.

Melt the butter in a large pan over medium heat. Slice the casing off the sausage and crumble the raw meat into the pan. I used fresh chorizo because it's easy to find in my neighborhood and I love the spicy, smoky flavor, but you should use whatever your favorite is. A sweet Italian sausage would taste great too. Sauté the meat until it's no longer pink, then move it to a large bowl.

Sauté the onion and garlic in the same pan, with the sausage drippings. Once the onion turns translucent, add the cabbage and sauté for 5 to 7 minutes, until tender enough to jab easily with a fork. Season generously with salt and pepper.

While the cabbage cooks, mix the rice and lentils into the sausage bowl. Add salt, pepper, and any other spices you'd like. I'd suggest repeating whatever spices are in the sausage: in the case of chorizo, that was paprika, cumin, and dried chilies, but if you were using Italian sausage, you might add some fennel seeds. Make sure you taste the mixture as you season it. If both parts of the casserole are tasty, you'll end up with a delicious meal. If they aren't seasoned well, it'll be bland.

Lightly oil a large casserole dish. Spread the lentil-rice-sausage mixture into an even layer. Next, spread the cabbage mixture on top. Then, as evenly as possible, pour the puréed tomatoes over top. Sprinkle with salt and pepper.

Bake until hot and bubbly, approximately 30 minutes.

Savory Summer Cobbler

FOR FOUR

Celebrate summer's most ubiquitous vegetables, tomato and zucchini, with a crunchy Southern biscuit topping.

3-4 medium zucchini or summer squash, chopped into bite-sized pieces

3-4 large tomatoes, canned or fresh, chopped into bite-sized pieces

3 cloves garlic, finely chopped

4 scallions, finely chopped

1 lemon, zested

¼ cup fresh basil (optional)

1 tbsp olive oil

salt and pepper

TOPPING

1½ cups all-purpose or whole-wheat flour

½ cup cornmeal

1 tbsp baking powder

½ tsp salt

1 tsp black pepper

1 tsp smoked paprika

½ cup sharp cheddar, grated

½ cup butter

1 cup milk

Put the butter for the topping in the freezer for 30 minutes. Set the oven to 425 °F.

Lightly oil an 8" x 10" baking dish (or any baking dish that will accommodate the mixture) and pile in the vegetables, garlic, scallions, lemon zest, and basil. Pour the olive oil, salt, and pepper over top and mix it up with your hands. Bake the vegetables for 25 minutes while you prepare the biscuit topping.

For the topping, measure out the flour, cornmeal, baking powder, salt, pepper, paprika, and cheese into a bowl. Mix it up!

Once the butter is frozen, use a box grater to flake the butter into the flour mixture. Gently massage the butter into the flour with your fingers until it's crumbly but still clumpy. Add the milk and quickly bring the dough together. Don't knead the dough: lumpiness is fine and results in flaky topping. Put it in the fridge until the vegetables come out of the oven.

Once the vegetable mixture has cooked for 25 minutes, quickly top it with small clumps of biscuit dough. The vegetables should still be visible in some areas.

Bake for 20 to 25 minutes or until the vegetables are bubbly and the topping is lightly browned. Top with some more cheddar and some chopped herbs, then enjoy!

For a variation, swap the zucchini for eggplant. Chop the eggplant into bite-sized pieces, salt them, and set them aside for 30 minutes before continuing with the recipe as you would with the zucchini.

$8 TOTAL
$2 / SERVING

$6.60 TOTAL
$1.65 / SERVING

Cauliflower Cheese

FOR FOUR

This is a classic side dish in Great Britain: creamy, cheesy sauce over cauliflower, baked in the oven until the edges get crunchy and bubbly. It's like a healthier and more flavorful version of macaroni and cheese. Alternatively, try this with broccoli or cooked winter squash—everyone will love it.

1 head cauliflower, cut into bite-sized florets
2 tsp salt
1 tbsp butter
3 cloves garlic, finely chopped
½ tsp chili flakes
1 bay leaf
1 tbsp all-purpose flour
1½ cups milk
6 oz sharp cheddar, grated
salt and pepper

ADDITIONS
breadcrumbs (p. 146)
1 tbsp Dijon mustard
4 scallions, finely chopped
1 lemon, zested
1 tsp smoked paprika
½ tsp thyme

Set the oven to 400 °F.

Bring a large pot of water to boil over high heat. Add the salt and the cauliflower, then leave it for 4 minutes.

Meanwhile, butter a baking dish large enough to comfortably accommodate all the cauliflower. I usually use a pie dish. Drain the water from the cauliflower and pour it into the baking dish.

To make the sauce, melt the butter in a saucepan on medium heat. Add the garlic, chili flakes, and bay leaf, then cook for about 1 minute. Add the flour and stir quickly. The flour-butter mixture is called a roux. You want the roux to get just a little brown; this will probably take another minute. Slowly add the milk to the pot, stirring all the while to incorporate the roux. Bring the sauce to a boil, stirring every now and then to make sure the sauce doesn't get scorched on the bottom. Once it comes to a boil, turn off the heat and stir in the cheese. Drop in any additions at this point. Taste the sauce and add salt and pepper as needed. You should have a creamy, smooth, savory sauce.

Pour the sauce over the cauliflower. Place the dish in the oven for 40 minutes, or until the top is brown and bubbly. You can also add some breadcrumbs to the top of the dish before baking if you like extra crunch.

Enjoy with a green salad. I also like mine with salsa.

Vegetable Quiche, Hold the Crust

FOR FOUR

Much as I love this quiche hot, I like it even better cold out of the fridge the next day. It makes a great fast breakfast or lunch. The quiche in the picture uses broccoli, but you can make it with pretty much any kind of vegetable. Some of my favorites are roasted green chilies and cheddar, winter squash with goat cheese, zucchini and tomato, or spinach and olive.

1 tbsp butter
1 large onion, sliced into half moons
3-4 cups chopped vegetables
8 eggs
1 cup milk
1 cup cheddar or other cheese, grated
1 tsp salt
½ tsp black pepper

Set the oven to 400 °F.

There are two ways to make this quiche. If you have a cast-iron or other oven-proof skillet, you can make the quiche right in the skillet. This cuts down on dishes. Otherwise, start with a regular skillet and later transfer everything to a pie plate to bake.

Melt the butter in a skillet over medium heat. Add your onion slices and sprinkle a bit of salt and pepper over them. Cook the onions until they are golden brown and starting to caramelize. If your pan is oven-proof, simply remove it from the heat and spread the onions evenly across the bottom. Otherwise, butter a pie plate and scoop the onions into it, creating an even layer on the bottom. The onions add a crust-like texture and a bit of crunch.

A note on vegetables: For things like broccoli, cauliflower or winter squash, I suggest steaming or cooking them before adding them to the quiche to ensure they'll be fully cooked. For tomatoes, zucchini, spinach or any other quick-cooking vegetable, just use them fresh.

Spread the vegetables evenly over top of the onions. The dish or pan should look fairly full.

In a bowl, use a fork to lightly beat the eggs with the milk, cheese, salt, and pepper, just enough to break up the yolks and whites. This is a savory custard mixture. Pour the custard over the vegetables and onions and enjoy watching it fill in all the free spaces.

Bake the quiche in the oven for 1 hour. Once the surface is lightly brown all the way across, it's fully cooked.

Let the quiche cool for about 20 minutes, then slice into wedges and serve with a side salad.

$12 TOTAL
$3 / SERVING

Shrimp and Grits

FOR FOUR

The cost of shrimp has jumped sharply since I wrote this recipe, so save this one until you can find a deal—under about $8 per pound. This is far from an authentic Southern version of this dish, but it is absolutely delicious. Southerners will demand you use white stone-ground corn for this, and I won't quibble, but feel free to use yellow if it doesn't offend you.

GRITS

1 cup grits
4½ cups vegetable or chicken stock
½ cup sharp cheddar, grated
3 scallions, finely chopped

TOPPING

1 lb shrimp, peeled and deveined
1 tbsp butter or vegetable oil
1 medium onion, chopped
1 bell pepper, chopped
2 sticks celery, chopped
2 cloves garlic, finely chopped
1 green chili, finely diced (optional)
1 tomato, chopped

Bring the stock to a boil in a medium-sized pot, then turn the heat down to low and slowly pour in the cornmeal while stirring briskly with a wooden spoon. Stirring while pouring is crucial to keep the grits creamy and smooth—no lumps! Once the grits become smooth and thick, place a lid on the pot with the spoon still in it so that steam can escape.

Let the grits cook while you prepare the rest of the meal, checking in occasionally to give them a stir. The total cooking time should be about 25 to 30 minutes.

Meanwhile, prepare the shrimp and vegetables. Add the butter or oil to a large pan on medium heat and let it get hot. Add the onion, pepper, and celery. Sauté until the onion is just translucent, about 2 minutes. Add the garlic, as well as the green chili if you like things spicy. Let everything cook for another minute. Add the tomato and cook for 3 or 4 minutes, until the tomato releases its juice and the vegetables resemble a thick and chunky sauce. Add a dribble of water to keep everything loose and saucy, then toss in the shrimp. Cook, stirring occasionally, until the shrimp are pink all over. Add salt and pepper to taste.

Once the grits are ready, take them off the heat and add the cheese and most of the scallions, then stir. Ladle the grits into bowls and top with the shrimp, vegetables, and a few more scallions.

Spicy, Crunchy, Creamy Polenta

FOR TWO

Polenta plus vegetable plus egg equals satisfying and delicious. You can also add a can of corn to the polenta for deep, rich, corny flavor. Or go a little different by adding frozen peas, scallions, olives, or (my favorite) green chilies to the polenta. Or skip the Romano and add ¼ cup of grated cheddar to the polenta.

½ cup polenta or cornmeal

2 cups water

½ tsp salt

1 tbsp olive oil

4 cups fresh spinach or 1 cup frozen spinach, roughly chopped

3 cloves garlic, finely chopped

1 anchovy, finely chopped (optional)

½ tsp chili flakes (or fresh chili)

2 eggs

Romano or Parmesan, freshly grated

salt and pepper

Bring the water and salt to a boil in a medium-sized pot, then turn the heat down to low and slowly pour in the polenta while stirring briskly with a wooden spoon. Stirring while pouring is crucial to keep the polenta creamy and smooth—no lumps! Once the cornmeal becomes smooth and thick, place a lid on the pot with the spoon still in it so that steam can escape.

Let the polenta cook while you prepare the rest of the meal, checking in occasionally to give it a stir. The total cooking time should be about 25 to 30 minutes, but if you're in a rush, you can eat it after 15.

Meanwhile, chop the spinach, garlic, and anchovy if you're using it. Set them aside. Add a bit of olive oil or butter to a pan on medium heat. Let the pan heat up until it sizzles when you flick it with water. Add the garlic, anchovy, and chili flakes. Let them cook until you can smell them, about 1 minute. Add the spinach and toss it around with a spoon or tongs, or just swirl the pan to coat the spinach with the garlic mixture. Let everything cook for 3 to 5 minutes, until the spinach is wilted. Remove the pan from the heat and move its contents to a bowl to wait for the polenta and eggs.

When the polenta is about 2 minutes from done, start with the eggs. Wipe the pan quickly with a cloth, then put it back on medium heat. Splash a bit more olive oil in the pan and wait for it to get hot. Crack the two eggs into the pan and cover with a lid. This will steam them, making sunny-side-up eggs with fully cooked whites.

Scoop the polenta into a pair of bowls. Add some Romano and lots of salt and pepper. Layer about half the vegetables over the polenta.

Once the whites of the eggs are cooked, remove them from the pan with a spatula and lay them over the polenta and vegetables. Top with the rest of the vegetables and further sprinklings of cheese.

$3.50 TOTAL
$1.75 / SERVING

$8 - $15 TOTAL
$1.50 - $2.75 / SERVING

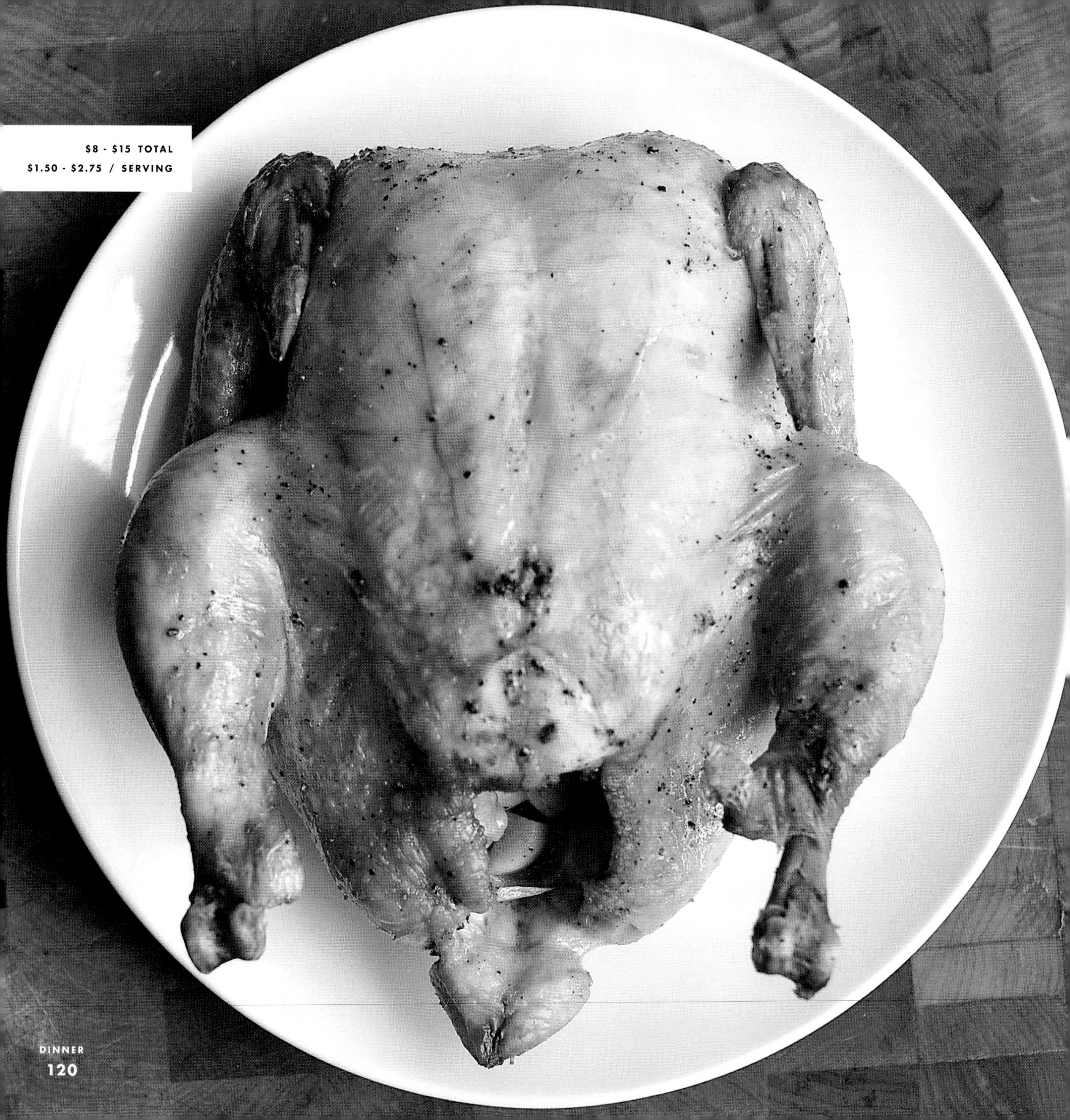

Roast Chicken

FOR SIX

A whole chicken is usually less expensive than buying single pieces like breasts or thighs—plus you can make stock later from the bones and any meat too difficult to get off. The leftovers can be used in sandwiches, tacos, over a salad, or tossed with sauce and mixed into pasta. This is a base recipe: add spices to the butter or sprinkle over the surface of the chicken to change up the flavor in any way you like.

1 whole chicken
1 tbsp butter
2 cloves garlic
1 lemon
   salt and pepper

Heat the oven to 400 °F.

Remove the giblets and neck from the chicken. Keep them for stock later. Rub the entire bird with butter, then sprinkle it with salt and pepper.

Smash the garlic cloves with the side of your knife and slice the lemon in half. Stuff the garlic and lemon into the chicken's body cavity.

Place the chicken in a roasting pan or an oven-proof skillet. Let it cook for 1 hour. If you have a meat thermometer, check to make sure the chicken is at 165 °F, the temperature when chicken is completely safe to eat. But 1 hour should be long enough to fully cook it.

Let the chicken rest for at least 10 minutes before you carve it to make sure you don't lose any of the tasty juices.

After you've carved away all the meat, make chicken stock from the carcass. Simmer it for several hours in a pot full of water along with scrap vegetables like the ends of onions and carrots, plus a generous helping of salt.

Set the oven to 400 °F.

Clean and chop your vegetables. Generally, I prefer to leave the skin on for the following reasons: skin tastes nice and gets crispy; there's a lot of nutrition in the skin; peeling is slow! Just be sure to wash the vegetables thoroughly.

It's up to you how you want to chop your vegetables. Many are nice roasted whole, like new potatoes or little sunchokes or turnips—they will be crispy and salty on the outside and bursting with fluffy, starchy goodness inside. The general rule is that the smaller you chop things, the faster they cook, so try to keep everything about the same size so nothing cooks faster than anything else.

Dump your vegetables into a roasting pan. Drizzle everything with olive oil or melted butter—about 2 tablespoons per medium-sized roasting pan. Season generously with salt and pepper and add any other extras from the list at right. Use your hands to coat the vegetables thoroughly with the oil and spices.

Pop the pan in the oven for 1 hour or longer, but check on the vegetables after 45 minutes. Test them by poking them with a knife. If it meets no resistance, they're finished; if not, let them cook longer. Don't worry: it's not much of a problem if you overcook them. Unlike vegetables overcooked through boiling or steaming, overcooked roasted vegetables may dry out a bit, but still retain their shape and flavor.

After you pull the vegetables out of the oven, push them around with a spatula to free them from the pan. Remove any garlic cloves and smash them into a fine paste (removing the skins at this point), then put the garlic back in the pan and mix together.

Squeeze the juice out of any lemons and discard the woody bits of any cooked herbs. Add a little more butter, a bit of favorite sauce, a little soft cheese or mayonnaise, and serve.

Turn the page for another great idea for roasted veggies.

METHOD

Roasted Vegetables

When the weather turns cool, I want only to eat warm, flavorful food. Roasting is easy, it warms up the kitchen, and it makes the house smell like the holidays. If you're uncertain how to prepare a new vegetable, you usually can't go wrong with roasting— most things end up sweeter, with nice crunchy bits. If you roast a bunch of vegetables at the beginning of the week, you can eat them throughout the week in various ways: with eggs at breakfast, folded into an omelette, as a side dish, in a taco or sandwich, on toast, or with any grain.

vegetables
olive oil or butter
salt and pepper

ROOTS

potatoes, sweet potatoes, beets, turnips, onions, parsnips, carrots, sunchokes, kohlrabi, fennel

NON-ROOTS

bell peppers, winter squash, broccoli, Brussels sprouts, cauliflower, asparagus, eggplant

EXTRAS

whole garlic cloves (unpeeled), lemon slices or lemon zest, anything you would pair with roast chicken, tough herbs like sage, oregano, thyme, bay leaves, any dry spice combination (p. 166)

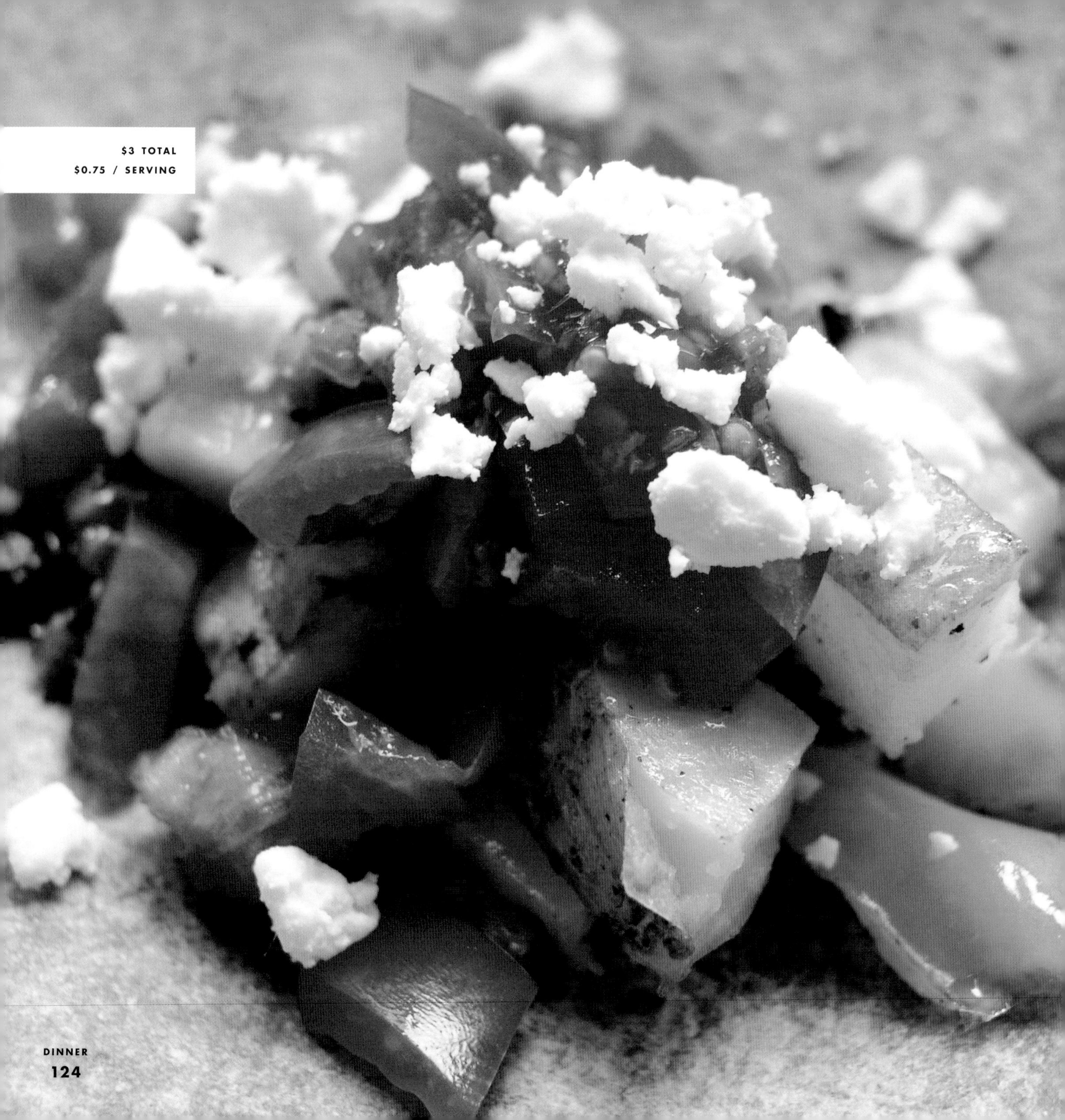

$3 TOTAL
$0.75 / SERVING

Roasted Potatoes with Chilies

FOR FOUR

It doesn't get much simpler or more satisfying than this. You can use any pepper you like—from large, dark poblanos, to Hungarian wax chilies, to bell peppers.

4 medium potatoes, chopped into bite-sized pieces
4 medium chilies, chopped into bite-sized pieces
2 cloves garlic, unpeeled
1 tbsp butter, melted
salt and pepper

In a large roasting pan, tumble together the potatoes, peppers, and garlic. When you chop the peppers, be sure to get rid of the seeds and white placenta inside.

Pour the butter over top and sprinkle liberally with salt and pepper. Potatoes need quite a bit of salt! Use your hands to mix everything up.

Roast for 1 hour, or until you can spear the potatoes easily with a fork and everything is a little crispy. Squish the garlic cloves, discard their skins, and spread the roasted garlic throughout.

In addition to being a great side dish, this makes a delicious taco filling. At left, it's pictured on a tortilla topped with chopped tomato and queso blanco.

Alternatively, try it alongside some black beans and rice or piled high on a plate with an egg on top.

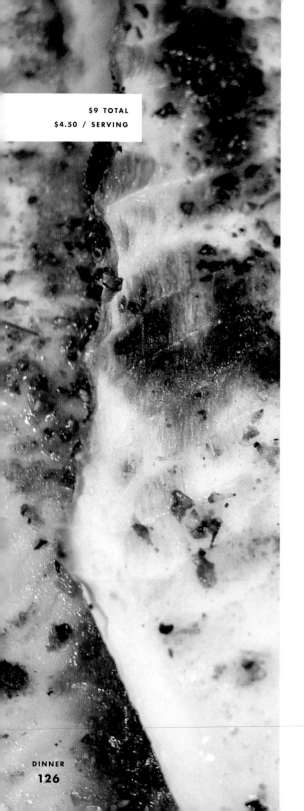

$9 TOTAL
$4.50 / SERVING

Spicy Broiled Tilapia with Lime

FOR TWO

This meal comes together so quickly it's astonishing. Broiled fish is crispy on the outside and flaky and moist on the inside. If you quickly sauté some vegetables while the fish cooks, dinner will be on the table in minutes.

2 fillets tilapia or other white fish
1 tsp salt
½ tsp pepper
1 tsp cayenne pepper

1 tsp cumin powder
½ tsp garlic powder
½ tsp oregano
½ lime, juiced

Turn your oven's broiler to high.

Mix the spices together in a small bowl. Sprinkle them over both sides of the fish and massage gently with your fingers to cover thoroughly in the spices.

Lay the fish on a baking pan lined with aluminum foil.

Broil for 4 to 7 minutes. The fish will cook very quickly, so after 4 minutes, check to see if they're done by gently inserting a butter knife into the thickest part. If it goes through easily and the fish flakes apart, you're done. If the knife meets resistance and the fish stays together, put the fillets back under the broiler for another few minutes. Once you've done this once or twice, you'll be able to tell when your fish is done at a glance.

When the fish is done, squeeze a lime over it. Serve with rice or a favorite side dish like spicy green beans (p. 59).

Big Batch

It's simple economics: usually making a large amount of something is cheaper and more efficient than making lots of different small dishes. You can blow a whole batch all on a big celebration or portion these dishes out and freeze them for later use. You'll be extremely grateful to your past self when you pull delicious home-made food out of the freezer on a busy Monday evening!

Spicy
Pulled
Pork

FOR TEN

$14 TOTAL
$1.40 / SERVING

Pulled pork is a celebration, worthy of a special day. It's incredibly flavorful, rich, spicy, and remarkably versatile. Although it seems expensive, it's quite a bargain when you look at the price per serving. As with most celebratory meals, this one takes quite a long time to prepare. Most of the time, however, is just spent waiting for it to cook "low and slow."

5 lb pork shoulder	3 tsp sweet paprika
	2 tsp cumin powder
DRY RUB	1 tsp coriander powder
1/3 cup brown sugar	1 tsp clove powder
2 tbsp coffee, ground	1 tsp garlic powder
2 tbsp kosher salt	1 tsp black pepper
4 tsp smoked paprika	

Mix the rub ingredients together. Apply liberally to the pork shoulder, pressing it gently into the meat until you've covered every side. Set any leftover rub aside for later. Place the pork shoulder in a large pot with a tight lid or a Dutch oven. Cover with a towel or lid and leave in the fridge for a few hours or overnight.

Pour enough water into the pot to cover the bottom. This will keep the juices from burning. Put the lid on and place the pot in a 200 °F oven for 10 to 12 hours. I find it's easier if I cook the pork overnight and pull it out in the morning, but you can put it in early in the morning and have it ready for dinner as well.

The supposed rule is that cooking takes 1.5 to 2 hours per pound of pork, but I find it usually takes a little longer than that. You are waiting for the internal temperature to reach 200 °F. The meat is edible at 160 °F, but at higher temperatures the tough connective tissues break down to create the flavor and texture that make pulled pork a delicious and unique treat.

If you don't have a meat thermometer, figuring out the internal temperature is obviously difficult, but you can test it by feel. Poke the meat with a finger: when it's so soft that it falls apart on its own, take it out of the oven.

To pull the meat, remove it from the juices and gently tear the pork apart with two forks or with your hands. Discard any larger bits of fat that you don't wish to eat. If any section is hard to tear apart, the meat hasn't cooked enough to break down the connective tissue. If you have the time to spare, put it back in the oven for another couple of hours.

Once you've pulled all of the pork, mix in any remaining rub and move it to a casserole dish or a large plate. If you aren't eating the meat right away, stash it in the fridge.

Optionally, if you want to make a sauce from the pot full of drippings, bring it to a gentle boil on the stovetop over medium-high heat. Let the juices thicken for 20 to 30 minutes. The fat will rise to the top: it's the clear, thick layer, not the thin, red liquid below. Skim off as much of the fat as possible. Mix a few spoonfuls of the pan drippings with the pork before serving.

Feel free to add a little barbecue sauce to the pork if it isn't flavorful enough for you, but try it first—I think you'll be surprised!

There are a million ways to eat pulled pork, but I like it over squishy hamburger buns or in tacos with crunchy vegetables. Traditionally, pulled pork sandwiches have cabbage slaw on them, but anything crunchy will do. (A diner near my apartment does a great slaw with apple and celery root.)

Don't forget some veggies on the side to round out the meal—a simple green salad, corn on the cob, steamed green beans, or any other summery vegetable.

Deviled Eggs

MAKES TWENTY-FOUR HALF EGGS

Deviled eggs are my favorite party food and the perfect recipe to dedicate to my friend Camilla. At parties, I often eat too much random junk food and end up feeling gross. These eggs are a great antidote: festive and delicious without being empty calories. Although they're a little fussy, they aren't actually difficult to make. I'll start you off with these few ideas, but you can add whatever flavors suit your fancy.

Hard-boiled eggs are easier to peel if the eggs aren't quite fresh, so try making these when you have eggs that have been sitting around for a week or two.

Place a layer of eggs at the bottom of a pot that is large enough to fit them with a bit of wiggle room. If you can't fit all your eggs, don't stack them—they might crack. Split them into batches instead.

Cover the eggs with cold water. Bring the pot to a boil over medium heat without a lid. As soon as the water is boiling, turn off the heat and cover the pot with a tight lid. Set a timer for 10 minutes.

When the timer goes off, gently pour out the hot water and cover the eggs with very cold water. The cold water stops the cooking process so that you don't end up with that slightly icky blue-green skin around your yolk.

Peel the eggs. Everyone has their own technique, but I like to gently roll each egg across the counter to crack the shell. Roll the egg around until it looks like a cracked desert landscape, then peel it starting from the bottom. Once peeled, rinse the egg and set it aside. Repeat until you have peeled all the eggs.

Slice each egg in half lengthwise. Pop the yolks out and put them in a medium bowl. Don't worry if you leave a little yolk behind. Set the whites aside on a plate.

Sprinkle the yolks with salt and pepper, then add other ingredients of your choice to the bowl. Mash with a fork and mix until it becomes a relatively smooth paste.

Arrange the whites on a plate and spoon the yolk mixture back into each hole. Pile the filling high! Alternatively, scoop the filling into a plastic sandwich bag. Cut off the corner of the sandwich bag and squeeze the yolk mixture into the whites.

Sprinkle with the scallions and some paprika for color. Have a great party!

12 eggs
    salt and pepper
2 scallions, finely chopped (optional)
    paprika (optional)

CLASSIC

2 tbsp mustard
2 tbsp mayonnaise
2 tbsp water, pickle juice, or lemon juice

CHILI AND LIME

2 tbsp mayonnaise
2 tbsp lime juice
1 jalapeno, finely chopped

CURRIED

2 tbsp mayonnaise
2 tbsp water
4 tsp curry powder or 1 tsp each of turmeric, cayenne, coriander, and cumin

RAMEN-INSPIRED

2 tbsp mayonnaise
2 tbsp soy sauce
1 tbsp cup rice vinegar
    chili sauce

TOMATO

2 tbsp mayonnaise
¼ cup fresh or canned tomato, finely chopped, or tomato sauce (p. 142)

CHORIZO

2 tbsp mayonnaise
2 tbsp fresh chorizo, cooked
1 tsp paprika

VARIATIONS

any spice combination (p. 166)
any vegetable, finely chopped
green chili and cheese
feta and fresh dill
bacon
avocado
olives

$3.60 TOTAL
$0.15 / HALF EGG

Perogies

MAKES SIXTY TO SEVENTY-TWO

This is a huge recipe that will feed you for days. It takes time and effort, but the results are worth it. The most fun approach is to invite a couple of friends over for a perogy-making party. Everyone takes home a bag or two for the freezer, and it's a great time!

DOUGH
4½ cups all-purpose flour
2 tsp salt
2 cups yogurt or sour cream
2 eggs
1 tbsp water, as needed

FILLING
5 Russet potatoes, roughly cubed
1½ cups sharp cheddar, shredded
salt and pepper

ADDITIONS
2 tbsp scallions, chopped
4 cloves roasted garlic, minced
2 tbsp Dijon mustard
1 tsp cayenne pepper
1 tsp paprika

TO SERVE
sour cream
scallions, chopped

In a large bowl, mix the flour and salt. Pour in the yogurt, eggs, and a tablespoon of water. Mix it slowly and carefully. The dough will be quite sticky. Cover it with a towel or plastic wrap while you make the filling.

Put the chopped potatoes in a pot and cover with water, then add a bit of salt. Cover with a lid and bring to a boil over medium-high heat before removing the lid. Let the potatoes cook until tender, about 20 minutes. Test them with a fork: if it goes through easily, they're done.

Drain the potatoes and add shredded cheese, salt, pepper, and any additions you might enjoy. I like strong aged cheese because you don't have to use as much. I usually use several additions, and you should play around with some of your favorite things—there aren't many flavors that don't work in potatoes! Next, mash the potatoes with an electric mixer or just two forks. Once the filling is ready, gather some friends because shaping takes some time!

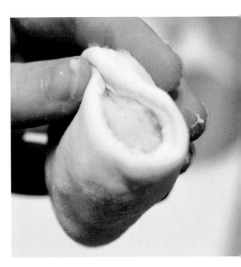

Flour your countertop liberally. Split the dough in half. Keep one half covered, but place the other half on the floured surface. Use a rolling pin to flatten the dough, about ¼" thick. Punch out as many 3" to 4" dough circles as possible, using a round cookie cutter or a drinking glass. Squish the scraps into the remaining covered half of the dough.

Drop about a tablespoon of filling in the center of one circle of dough. Fold the dough over the filling and press the edges to create a dumpling. The stickiness should ensure a tight seal. Lay the dumpling on a floured surface and use a fork to squish the edges together. Repeat until you run out of circles, then repeat everything with the remaining dough.

Once you have all your perogies formed, boil a pot of water and add about 12 perogies. Let them cook until they rise to the top, about 1 minute. Pull out the boiled perogies with a spoon, then repeat with the remainder in the same pot of water.

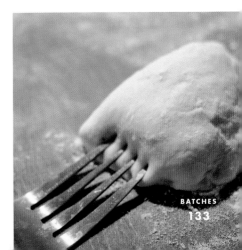

If you're planning to freeze some of the perogies, let them cool down and then put them in freezer bags with the air squeezed out. I usually do 12 to a bag, but you can portion them out in whatever way suits you. They will keep for at least 6 months in the freezer.

You can eat the perogies just boiled, but if you're anything like my family, you'll prefer them fried afterwards. Melt a tablespoon of butter in a pan on medium heat, then fry up as many perogies as you want. (Six per person is plenty.) Flip them every few minutes until they're browned on all sides. Serve with scallions and a dollop of sour cream.

$7.20 TOTAL
$0.12 / DUMPLING

Dumplings

MAKES SIXTY

DOUGH

4 cups flour

salt

2 eggs

1 cup water

VEGGIE FILLING

3 cups broccoli,
finely chopped

2 cups carrot, grated

8 oz firm tofu, crumbled

2 tbsp soy sauce

1 tsp toasted sesame oil

2 scallions, chopped

2 eggs

PORK FILLING

1 lb ground pork
or sausage,
cooked or raw

3 cups collards, chard,
spinach, or scallions,
finely chopped

2 tbsp soy sauce

1 tsp toasted sesame oil

2 scallions, chopped

2 eggs

ADDITIONS

ginger root, grated

garlic

My friend Raffaella comes from a huge family and fondly recalls making dumplings with her sisters growing up. (Her brothers just ate them.) Dumplings are a great way to use up veggies that don't look fresh anymore. Minced inside a dumpling, they come back to life! I've provided a couple of ideas here, but as with so many recipes, the filling is up to you. If you mess up and it comes out bland, just dip the dumpling in soy sauce or chili sauce and you'll still be happy.

To save time, see whether your grocery store has pre-made dumpling wrappers, usually in the freezer section or Asian aisle. They come round or square and might be called gyoza or wonton wrappers, but any will work.

If you're making your own dumpling dough, add the flour and salt to a large bowl. Make a crater in the middle and crack in the eggs along with the water. Use one hand like a shovel to mix the dough into a shaggy mass. If it seems too dry, add water a few drops at a time. Knead the dough for a minute, then cover it with plastic wrap or a damp towel and let it rest for 30 minutes to 2 hours.

Choose one filling or the other. Mix all the filling ingredients in a large bowl.

Once the dough has rested, split it into four chunks. Dust your countertop with flour, then roll the first piece of dough into a log. Leave the other pieces covered so that they don't dry out.

Cut the log into 15 equal slices, then use your hands to form one of the slices into a flat disc. With a rolling pin, flatten the disc into an almost paper-thin circle about the size of a drink coaster.

Place a heaping tablespoon of filling in the center of the dough. Lift all the edges to meet in the middle, then pinch it closed like a little parcel. If the dough won't stick to itself, wet your fingertips and dab the edges.

Repeat until you run out of either filling or dough. This is a great time to ask for help from family or friends—one person rolling while others fill and cook.

Now, a tough decision: do you want to steam, fry, or boil your dumplings?

To steam them, spread a small amount of oil around a large pan. Fill the pan with dumplings—as many as you can fit without them sticking to each other. Turn the heat to medium and let them sizzle for about a minute. Once the dough has absorbed most of the oil, add about ½ cup of water to the pan, then quickly cover with a lid. The water will splatter and sizzle loudly. Leave the lid on for 5 minutes to steam the dumplings, then turn the heat down to low and remove the lid. Let it keep cooking until the water evaporates, then turn off the heat. Your dumplings should be steamed on top with crispy, brown bottoms.

To pan-fry them instead, start following the technique above, but use more oil. Skip the water and the lid entirely. Just keep frying! Once the dumplings are golden on one side, flip them to fry the other side. This method is awkward with parcel-style dumplings but works well for other shapes, so plan accordingly.

Alternatively, boil the dumplings by dropping them into a pot of boiling water. When they rise to the top, they're ready to eat, usually in 1 or 2 minutes.

Staples

These are the building blocks of great meals. Freshly made flatbreads are amazingly cheap to produce and taste fabulous. They can take a bit of time to make at first, but you'll get faster with practice and the flavor is absolutely worth it. Large batches of grains and beans can be cooked at the beginning of the week, then used in different meals each day, saving both time and money. Staples are where the possibilities begin!

DAL GREEN LENTILS ARBORIO RICE CHICKPE

Flour Tortillas

MAKES TWENTY-FOUR SMALL

$1.70 TOTAL
$0.07 / TORTILLA

Homemade tortillas are a bit of work, but they're totally worth it. With practice, you'll get quicker and enjoy the process as much as the results.

1¼ cups all-purpose flour
1¼ cups whole-wheat flour
2½ tsp baking powder
1 tsp salt
⅓ cup clarified butter or lard
1 cup hot water

In a large bowl, whisk the dry ingredients. Add clarified butter or lard. Lard is more traditional, but I prefer clarified butter. Even regular butter is fine. Using your fingers, squish the butter against the flour until the mixture looks like moist crumbs. Add the hot water—not boiling, just hot—and form into dough with your hands. Leave the dough in the bowl for an hour, covered by plastic wrap or a moist towel.

Roll the dough into 24 small balls. Keep them covered with the towel.

Lightly flour your countertop. Gently flatten one dough ball with your palm, then roll it out with a rolling pin. Flip it over to make sure it doesn't stick to the counter; add more flour if it does stick. Once you have the ball rolled out nice and thin, set it aside under a moist towel.

Once you've rolled out one or two tortillas, put a non-stick or cast-iron pan on medium-high heat. Let it get nice and hot. Place a tortilla in the pan. Once it starts to dry up around the edges, flip it over with a spatula, then gently press it down to give it some color underneath. Once the tortilla has brown spots on both sides, remove it from the pan and continue with the next. Work quickly! As you wait for each tortilla to cook, roll out more. You'll get better at this part with practice.

If you're serving the tortillas soon, place them in a warm oven to keep them pliable. If they're for later in the day, pile them under a cloth while you finish making them. Once you're done, wrap them in aluminum foil and put them in the fridge. Heat in the oven before serving.

Roti

MAKES SIXTEEN

These are a staple flatbread in many parts of India. They're quick to make and very tasty when fresh. Enjoy them with a curried filling, dip them in soups or stews, or fill them with eggs at breakfast.

2 cups whole-wheat flour
1 tsp salt
1 cup water

In a small bowl, mix together all the ingredients using one clean hand. It should form a fairly moist dough. Knead until smooth and form into a ball. Cover with a damp towel or paper towel and set aside for 10 minutes to an hour.

Divide the dough into 16 small balls.

Sprinkle a countertop with flour and place one piece of dough in the middle. Cover the ball with flour on all sides so that it doesn't stick to the surface, then gently roll it out with a rolling pin (or a bottle if you're in a pinch) until it's thin and flat, about ⅛" thick. As you roll the dough, be sure to unstick it from your counter and flip it over. To make it round, roll straight in front of you, then turn the dough 90 degrees and roll out again.

Place a non-stick skillet on medium heat. Once the pan is hot, add the roti and cook until the dough lifts away from the pan around the edges and small bubbles form. Flip the bread over and cook the other side. Usually it goes very quickly. You want to see light-brown bubbles all over the dough. Don't let it get too dark, though, as this will make the roti too crunchy to use for rolls. Repeat this process until you're finished with the dough.

Once you have practiced, you can roll out one roti while another cooks in the pan to make the process quicker.

Keep them under a towel on the counter or in a warm oven until ready to serve.

$0.50 TOTAL
$0.03 / ROTI

Pizza Dough

MAKES FOUR INDIVIDUAL PIZZAS

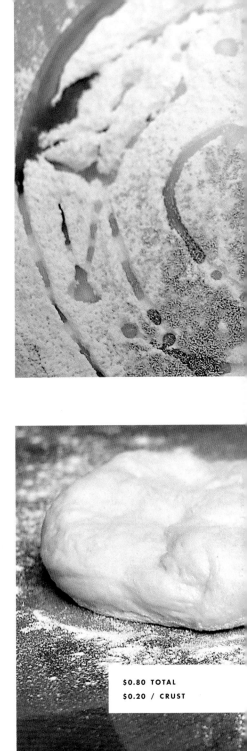

There are two ways to make pizza dough: the fast way and the slow way. They're the same amount of work, just with different waits. The slow method is convenient for a weekday if you make it before bed the night before, pop it in the fridge, then pull it out to rise before dinner.

3 cups all-purpose or bread flour
1½ tsp salt
½ to 1 tsp instant yeast
1 tbsp olive oil
1¼ cup water

FAST METHOD

Measure out the flour, salt and a teaspoon of yeast into a big bowl. Mix the oil into the flour with your hands, crumbling it until the texture is a bit sandy, then add the room-temperature water. Keep mixing with your hands until it comes together.

Knead the dough on a lightly floured countertop for 5 to 7 minutes, until it becomes a smooth elastic ball. The dough will be smooth but quite wet.

Add a small amount of oil to a bowl. Place your dough ball in the bowl and cover with plastic wrap. Let it rise for 1½ to 3 hours, depending on the warmth of your kitchen. It's done rising when it has doubled in size. Then it'll be ready to shape into your favorite pizza!

SLOW METHOD

If you're organized enough to make the slow dough, I recommend taking the extra time: it's the best.

Use the same process as at left, but add only ½ teaspoon of yeast to the flour mixture. Rather than room temperature, the water should be very cold.

After you place the dough ball in a bowl and cover it, put it into the fridge overnight. Letting the yeast work overnight creates a better flavor; it also makes the dough more elastic and easier to work with.

The next day, 2 to 3 hours before you want to bake your pizzas, remove the dough from the fridge to return to room temperature.

$0.80 TOTAL
$0.20 / CRUST

$0.35 TOTAL
$0.35 / SERVING

Fresh Pasta

FOR ONE LARGE ENTREE

¾ cup all-purpose flour
   or bread flour
1 egg
   olive oil or vegetable oil

When a reader, Jeanne, asked for a good pasta dish, I decided to show her how to create it from scratch. Sure, making pasta by hand requires elbow grease and a good rolling pin, but you'll be surprised at how simple, cheap, and tasty it is. If an Italian grandmother can do it, so can you! Because fresh pasta is so wonderful, the sauce doesn't need to be complicated. I love this with tomato sauce (p. 142) and a little cheese.

Multiply this recipe by the number of people you are serving, maybe a bit less. The stated quantities are a useful ratio, but produce big portions.

Put the flour in a bowl. Make a crater in the center of the flour and crack the egg into it. Mix with your hands. The egg takes a while to release all its moisture, so don't panic if things are dry at first. If, after mixing for about a minute, the dough still seems excessively dry, add a teaspoon of water. Keep mixing until you develop a stiff dough that is quite dry. The dryness makes it easier to roll out and keeps the noodles from sticking together when you cook them.

Place the dough in a lightly oiled bowl covered with a moist towel or plastic wrap for 1 or 2 hours.

Once an hour (or more) has passed, you'll notice a marked change in the dough. Now that the egg has released its moisture, you'll have a pale yellow, smooth, pliable dough. Knead again to create a smooth ball.

Tear or slice the dough into manageable pieces—usually as many as the number of people you're feeding. Dust your countertop or cutting board heavily with flour, then use a rolling pin to make the dough as thin as you can. Rolling it out will take a while because it's tough and stretchy. Try to get it thin enough to see light through. The thinner the dough, the quicker it will cook, but don't make the dough so thin that it tears.

By the time the pasta is rolled out, it should be dry enough to avoid sticking to itself. If it's still moist, leave it to sit for a few minutes.

Slice into whatever size of noodles you like. It's easy to make the noodles a consistent size if you fold the dough over itself a few times first. Shake the cut noodles on a tray with a bit of flour to keep them from sticking.

Boil in heavily salted water. Fresh pasta cooks in as little as 30 seconds if the noodles are thin. It's ready when it changes color and starts to float.

You can keep uncooked pasta for up to 2 days in the fridge.

Best Tomato Sauce

MAKES THREE AND A HALF CUPS

There are many ways to make tomato sauce. I don't find that the more complex recipes taste any better; this one is boldly tomatoey and works on just about anything. It also takes 5 minutes to make. Can't beat that.

1 tbsp olive oil
3 cloves garlic, finely chopped
½ tsp chili flakes
28 oz can tomatoes, crushed or diced
½ lemon, zested (optional)
salt and pepper

Add the olive oil to a saucepan on medium heat. Sauté the garlic for 1 minute, until it smells great and becomes translucent. Add the chili flakes and cook for 30 seconds. Add the can of tomatoes, mix, and cook until warmed through. Add a little lemon zest, then salt and pepper to taste. Since canned tomatoes are often already salted, you may not need to add any.

If you want a thicker sauce that will stick to pasta better, cook for 10 to 20 minutes to evaporate more of the liquid. Use immediately or keep in a jar in the fridge for later use.

$3.50 TOTAL
$1 / CUP

Chorizo and White Bean Ragu

MAKES THREE CUPS

When my friend Chris told me he loves a good ragu, I worked to develop a version that is as hearty as a meaty tomato sauce without the expense and heaviness of a traditional ragu. A batch of this is probably enough for four people, served with grated Romano or Parmesan over pasta (p. 141), polenta, or grits.

1 tbsp butter or vegetable oil
1 onion, chopped
3 cloves garlic, finely chopped
1 tbsp jalapeño, finely chopped (optional)
½ lb fresh chorizo, casing removed

1½ cups canned or fresh tomatoes, puréed
1½ cups butter beans, navy beans, or cannelini beans
salt and pepper

Melt the butter in a pan over medium heat and swirl it to coat the pan. Add the chopped onion and cook until it turns translucent. Toss in the garlic, jalapeño, and fresh chorizo (or any other kind of fresh sausage), then sauté for about a minute. Add the tomatoes and beans, then simmer until the sauce is thick and the sausage is cooked, about 5 minutes on medium heat. Taste and add salt and pepper as needed.

Because this sauce contains meat, it won't keep especially long in the fridge, but you can freeze it for later use if you don't plan to eat it all within a few days.

$3.75 TOTAL
$1.25 / CUP

$1.50 TOTAL
$0.75 / SERVING

Rainbow Rice

FOR TWO

Here are three quick ways to make plain rice a little more exciting. An early reader, Charles, said he loves rice with vegetables, but these treatments work for grains other than rice as well—everything from quinoa to barley to farro. Vegetables are a great way to liven up the usual rice and beans.

1 cup rice
2 cups water
salt

To make normal rice, pour 2 cups of water into a pot with 1 cup of uncooked rice and two pinches of salt. That'll be enough for two generous portions, or three or four smaller servings. With the lid off, bring to a low boil over medium heat, then turn the heat down to low and put the lid on slightly askew, so that the steam can escape. Cook for about 20 minutes, until the water is all gone.

1 cup canned
tomatoes, puréed

RED RICE: Stir the tomatoes with 1½ cups of water, then pour it into a pot with 1 cup of uncooked rice and two pinches of salt. Cook as above.

1 cup canned winter
squash, pumpkin, or
sweet potato, puréed

ORANGE RICE: Stir the squash, pumpkin, or sweet potato with 1½ cups of water, then pour it into a pot with 1 cup of uncooked rice and two pinches of salt. (You can also use frozen, boiled, or sautéed squash.) Cook as above.

1 cup frozen spinach,
beet greens, chard,
or fresh parsley

GREEN RICE: Chop up the spinach as much as you like. The more finely chopped, the more it will disperse into the rice. Cook normal rice, as above, for about 15 minutes, until most of the water is gone but not quite all. Mix the spinach into the rice. Cook with the lid off for the last 5 minutes. Adding the spinach at the end keeps it lush and bright, rather than the sad color of overcooked spinach.

How to Cook Dried Beans

The best way to prepare dried beans is to soak them overnight. The next day, drain the water and rinse thoroughly before cooking in fresh water.

If you didn't have the foresight to soak the beans ahead of time, you can make up for it. Cover the beans with water, then bring them to a boil in a large pot. After 10 minutes, take them off the heat and drain them. Proceed with the next step.

Cover the drained beans with fresh water in a large pot. Bring to a boil on medium heat, then turn down the heat so that the beans boil gently. Put a lid on the pot, but leave it askew so the water doesn't boil over.

Check on the beans every half hour or so, making sure to keep them covered with water if it boils away.

Beans take vastly different lengths of time to become tender. The older and bigger they are, the longer they take to cook. Very old, very large beans can take as long as four hours.

If you are making refried beans or beans for a soup or stew, don't worry about overcooking them; it's fine if they're mushy. If you want to maintain their shape and integrity, however, monitor them closely once they're getting close to done.

Once the beans are tender, you can drain them or leave them wet, depending on what you're using them for. Add salt to taste—they will need a fair bit!

ADDITIONS WHILE COOKING

a bay leaf

a bouquet garni of favourite tough herbs

dried herbs and spices

onion

garlic

chilies

ginger root

METHOD

Croutons or Breadcrumbs

bread
butter or vegetable oil as needed
salt and pepper

I am constantly haunted by the hard, several-day-old bread that I have neglected. Luckily there are plenty of delicious solutions that avoid the trash can. Croutons and breadcrumbs will keep for ages in a sealed container on the counter, and when you have them around you'll find yourself using them everywhere and finding excuses to make a salad.

This is a method more than a recipe since you'll have a random amount of bread. If making croutons, start by cutting the bread into cubes. If making breadcrumbs, mince the loaf with a knife, or just tear it apart, or throw small chunks of bread into a food processor. If the bread is too hard to cut, wrap it in a kitchen towel, sprinkle some water on the towel, and microwave for 20 to 30 seconds. This will restore just enough moisture to let you cut the bread easily.

Choose a sufficiently large pan for the quantity of bread cubes or crumbs—or work in batches if you have a lot—and place it on the stovetop on medium heat. Add enough butter or vegetable oil to coat the bottom of the pan. I prefer the flavor of butter, but use whatever you have.

Let the butter melt or the oil get hot. Add the bread and toss gently until coated. Let the bread sit for 2 minutes, then flip the pieces over. Keep tossing and turning until the bread is brown all over. Add oil or butter as needed and sprinkle with salt and pepper. It is basically impossible, unless you are very patient (which I am not) to get every side of the cubes browned, so just get them generally looking good and toasty and then take them off the heat.

For breadcrumbs, if you like, you can go oil-free: just toast whole slices and then crush it into small pieces.

Use the breadcrumbs or croutons immediately, or place them in a sealed container after letting them cooling off. Later, use them in salads or anything you want to add crunch to.

Drinks

You don't need a special drink at every meal (unless of course it is the meal!) but when you do, let fruit play a leading role, and make it yourself. It'll be so much better than the overpriced bottles in the supermarket.

Agua Fresca

SERVES FOUR TO SIX

Refreshing and hydrating, these beautiful drinks are great at a party, and they can help you use up any fruit that you won't be able to eat before it goes off. This is certainly not the master recipe, just a good starting point.

2 cups fruit, chopped
4 cups water

ADDITIONS
1 tsp vanilla
squeeze of lemon
or lime juice
sugar
mint leaves
other herb leaves

VARIATIONS
blueberry and lemon
cucumber and lemon
mango and lime
melon
orange
papaya
peach and vanilla
pineapple
strawberry and mint

For a very lightly flavored agua fresca, just mix the water and fruit together. Done! Obviously, if you want more fruit flavor, then use less water; if you want less flavor, then use more water.

I usually run my agua fresca through the blender, however. If you want the drink to be clear, strain the pulpy leftovers of the fruit after blending. If you're using blueberries or oranges or other fruit with a skin, you'll almost certainly want to strain it.

For some fruits, you can also choose to leave the pulp: it's particularly great when making a melon agua fresca since it mostly disappears.

Serve over ice. Try some of the variations I've suggested or whatever fruits you like!

Smoothies

FOR TWO

I have four types of smoothies here, but of course there are many more. Give these a try when you have overripe fruit that you wouldn't eat otherwise. Add a teaspoon of vanilla to any of these and they will seem incredibly professional. The frozen melon drinks, in particular, are the most refreshing treat on a hot summer day.

DRINKABLE YOGURT: If you like the grocery store's yogurt drinks, try making these at home for less! You don't even need to blend them—just add the juice and yogurt to a jar, then shake.

½ cup plain yogurt
½ cup fruit juice

MELON SMOOTHIE (TWO PICTURED): When you buy a melon, dice and freeze whatever you don't eat. Pull it out and blend it with a bit of water or juice to thin it out. It's like a better slushy!

1 cup frozen melon
½ cup water or juice
1 tsp vanilla

BERRY SMOOTHIE: Blend until smooth, then adjust with more berries or milk to your taste.

½ cup yogurt
1 cup frozen berries
 milk or juice to thin as needed

MANGO LASSI (NOT PICTURED): Blend the mango and yogurt together. If it's too thick to drink with a straw, add some milk to thin it out. A ripe and juicy mango combined with thin yogurt is often all you need. Be warned: if you make this for children, they will request it over and over.

1 mango, diced
1 cup yogurt
 milk to thin as needed

$1 - $2 TOTAL
$0.50 - $1 / SERVING

Desserts

Whether it's been a rough day, it's time to celebrate, or just because it's Wednesday, these sweets are totally worth it.

Caramelized Bananas

FOR TWO

These bananas—cooked in just a bit of caramel—are crispy and gooey on the outside and almost like a soft pudding inside. Sweet, messy, and irresistible.

2 bananas, peeled and split in half
1 tbsp butter
2 tbsp brown sugar

Melt the butter in a non-stick or cast-iron pan on medium-high heat. Add the sugar and let it melt into the butter for about 2 minutes. Place the bananas face down in the butter-sugar mixture, then cook for 2 minutes or until they become brown and sticky. Carefully flip them over and do the same to the other side.

Serve them whole or split them into quarters. Drizzle any caramel left in the pan over the bananas. Serve with ice cream or on their own.

$0.70 TOTAL
$0.35 / SERVING

$10 TOTAL

$0.25 / COOKIE

Coconut Chocolate Cookies

MAKES FORTY

A just-chewy-enough, just-crispy-enough, just-gooey-enough cookie that's perfect for a special treat.

- ²/₃ cup shaved, unsweetened coconut, toasted
- 1½ cups chocolate chips
- ½ lb unsalted butter (2 sticks)
- 2 cups all-purpose flour
- 1 tsp salt
- 1 tsp baking soda
- 1½ cups dark brown sugar
- 2 eggs
- 2 tsp vanilla

Heat the oven to 350 °F.

Spread the coconut into a thin, even layer on a cookie sheet. Place it in the oven for 5 to 8 minutes, until it's light brown, toasty, and aromatic.

Melt the butter in a heavy-bottomed saucepan over low heat. Once it's melted, leave it to cool in the pan for a few minutes.

In a medium-sized bowl, stir together the flour, salt, and baking soda.

In another bowl, beat the brown sugar and melted butter together for about 2 minutes, until they're smooth. Add the eggs and vanilla and beat for about 5 minutes, until the mixture lightens in color. Mix the flour mixture with the brown sugar mixture, a third at a time, until it forms a dark brown, homogeneous mass. Add the chocolate chips and coconut and stir until just combined.

Place the dough in the fridge for 20 minutes.

Afterwards, scoop tablespoons of dough onto a lightly buttered cookie sheet, leaving large spaces between each cookie so they have space to spread out. I usually do about 6 cookies per sheet. Just before putting the cookies into the oven, sprinkle them with salt.

Let the cookies bake for 8 to 10 minutes. After you take them out of the oven, leave them on the sheet to set for 2 minutes, then move them to plates to cool further. Don't stack the cookies until they've cooled fully.

Continue the process until the dough is gone.

Store the finished cookies in an airtight container.

Peach Coffee Cake

FOR TWELVE

This is adapted from the apple cake often served during Rosh Hashanah. It's simple and wonderful for dessert, with tea, or as a sweet breakfast. The juicy peaches add a ton of flavor to this simple cake. If you buy peaches in season, the cost can be quite reasonable.

6 peaches, pitted and cut into 8 slices each

1 tsp cinnamon

½ lemon, juiced

2 cups all-purpose flour

2 tsp baking powder

½ lb unsalted butter (2 sticks), at room temperature

1⅓ cups brown sugar

⅛ tsp salt

2 large eggs

1 tsp vanilla

Turn your oven to 350 °F.

Using the paper wrapping from the butter, lightly butter an 8" x 11" glass baking dish or 9" springform pan. Any shape will do so long as it is large enough. This cake doubles in size when it bakes.

In a large bowl, mix the peach slices, lemon juice, and cinnamon together with your hands, making sure the peaches are well coated in cinnamon.

In a medium bowl, stir the flour with the baking powder, getting rid of any lumps.

In another large bowl, beat the butter, brown sugar, and salt, either with a wooden spoon or an electric mixer. Stop when the mixture is fluffy and has slightly lightened in color. Add the vanilla, then the eggs one at a time, fully mixing in the first before adding the second.

If using an electric mixer, switch to a wooden spoon and add the flour mixture into the butter mixture, gently incorporating it until it's smooth. The batter will be quite thick.

Spread half the batter over the bottom of the buttered pan. Evenly distribute 24 of the peach slices over top. (There should be 48 in total.) Spread the other half of the batter over the peaches, then top with the remaining peaches. Sprinkle with a tablespoon or so of sugar and place the cake in the oven.

Bake for 1 hour or until a knife inserted into the center comes out clean.

$9 TOTAL
$0.75 / SERVING

Fast Melon Sorbet

FOR FOUR

2 cups frozen melon
½ cup plain yogurt
¼ cup sugar
1 tsp vanilla
or lime juice
(optional)

When you see lovely watermelons, honeydews, and cantaloupes on sale, buy them up. Eat half, then cube and freeze the other half. When you want a quick dessert or smoothie, pull out a bag of frozen melon and whip this up.

Add all the ingredients to a food processor or blender until just smooth. Don't blend too much, or the sorbet will become oversoft. Serve immediately or stick it into the freezer to enjoy later.

$2.40 TOTAL
$0.60 / SERVING

Avocado Milkshake

FOR TWO

John, the reader who introduced me to the silky magic of this milkshake, lives in California, where avocados are often less than a dollar. If you can find a similar deal, whip up a batch of these! If your avocado isn't quite ripe, a bit more lime juice will bring out the flavor.

1 avocado
2 cups milk
1 tsp vanilla
1 tbsp lime juice
1 pinch salt
2 tbsp sugar

Toss all the ingredients in a blender and whizz them up! Let it go for a while because the avocados need to break down and blend with the milk. Once the liquid is Kermit the Frog green, it's ready. Taste it and add more sugar or lime juice as needed.

These shakes are even better if you use "coconut milk beverage," almond milk, or rice milk instead of regular milk. Each adds a little of its own flavor to the drink.

$2.30 TOTAL
$1.15 / SERVING

Flavor

If you have a great sauce or a few spices in your kitchen, you'll never have to tolerate bland food. Most of these recipes require surprisingly little effort and time, pack a ton of flavor, and can be stored for use in any dish you choose.

Peanut Sauce

MAKES ONE CUP

$3 TOTAL
$3 / CUP

1 jalapeño or other chili, finely chopped (or 2 tbsp chili paste)

3 cloves garlic

1 shallot (or equivalent of any onion)
cooking oil

1 tsp turmeric (optional)

½ to 1 cup coconut milk

½ cup sugarless peanut butter

1 tbsp soy sauce

1 tbsp brown sugar (optional)

½ tsp sesame oil

Finely chop the pepper, garlic, and shallot, or use a food processor to make them into a paste. (If you're using chili paste instead of a fresh pepper, hold off on it for now.)

Splash some oil in a saucepan on medium heat. Once it's warm, add the chili, garlic, and shallot and sauté until everything's translucent. Add the turmeric, coconut milk, and chili paste if applicable.

Let it come to a boil, then turn the heat down. Add the peanut butter and soy sauce and stir to combine. Once it's all combined, taste it and add whatever you think it needs—but think about the salt and spice in particular.

$3.50 TOTAL
$3.50 / CUP

Spice Oil

MAKES ONE CUP

Use this spice oil on salads, in cold noodle dishes, or on roasted or sautéed vegetables. If you have trouble finding the spices, you can get all of them at most Asian grocery stores.

1 clove garlic
1 cup olive or vegetable oil
2 tbsp chili flakes or dried red chilies
1 tsp Sichuan or regular peppercorns
1 star anise
½ tsp cumin seeds
¼ tsp salt

Use the side of a knife to crush the garlic clove until it cracks open. Add all of the ingredients to a small pot.

Warm the mixture over low heat for about 10 minutes, until it starts to bubble gently and you can hear a bit of a sizzle, then turn off the heat. You want to heat it just enough to let the spices infuse into the oil, without getting so hot that the spices start to cook or fry.

Remove the pot from the stovetop and put it in the fridge with a lid. Let the spices infuse for 4 to 8 hours.

Taste the oil. If it isn't strongly spicy, let it infuse for a few more hours. Once it's ready, strain through a sieve to remove the spices.

Store in a jar in the fridge for up to a week.

$2.25 TOTAL
$0.75 / CUP

Salsa

MAKES THREE CUPS

Summertime salsas combine a load of fresh tomatoes with smaller amounts of choice vegetables and fruit. In the winter, cook canned tomatoes for a few minutes first.

2 cups tomatoes, chopped
½ medium onion, finely diced
1 jalapeño pepper, finely diced
1 lime, juiced
¼ cup fresh cilantro, finely chopped
salt and pepper

ADDITIONS
mango, peach, plum, or pineapple
beans
corn
garlic

Apart from its usual use on tortilla chips and tacos, this salsa is a wonderful topping for fish or chicken, as a sauce for cold noodles, or as a finishing touch on a savory breakfast.

If you like raw onion, go right ahead. Otherwise, take the edge off by sautéing the onion with a bit of water in a pan over medium heat. The onion is ready once the water has boiled off. If you aren't a fan of cilantro, substitute another herb: mint, savory, or lemon balm work well.

Mix the onion, tomato, and the rest of the ingredients in a bowl. Be sure to add enough salt and pepper!

Taste the salsa. You're looking for a balance of spicy from the peppers, sweet from the tomatoes, and bright and fresh from the herbs and lime juice. If something's out of balance, add the appropriate ingredient to bring it back into balance.

Store in an air-tight container in the fridge. Fresh salsa won't last as long as store-bought salsa because it doesn't have any preservatives, but it's so tasty that I'm sure you'll finish it fast!

$2.50 TOTAL
$1.25 / CUP

Raita

MAKES TWO CUPS

Raita is a traditional Indian sauce served with all kinds of things. It's simple and surprisingly tasty. Spoon it onto chana masala (p. 93), the potato and kale rolls (p. 84), or anything spicy to cool things down.

1 cup cucumber, chopped
½ cup tomato, chopped
¼ cup red onion, chopped
1 cup yogurt
1 tsp cumin powder
½ tsp cayenne powder
2 tbsp fresh cilantro, chopped
salt and pepper

ADDITIONS

1 tbsp ginger, grated
2 tbsp mint
¼ cup chickpeas
cooked spinach

This recipe is extremely loose. Basically, just stir some of your favorite chopped vegetables into yogurt and add salt and pepper. Use this as a stepping stone to develop your own.

After you stir all the ingredients together, store the raita in a covered container in the fridge until you're ready to use it.

$3.50 TOTAL
$1.75 / CUP

Tzatziki

MAKES TWO CUPS

If you're in a hurry, you don't have to strain this at all: you can just mix the ingredients together. However, removing the water from the cucumber and yogurt intensifies the flavor. Your patience will be rewarded by a thick sauce that gives you a new perspective on cucumbers.

2 cups yogurt
1 large cucumber, grated
1 tsp salt
2 tbsp fresh dill, chopped
2 scallions, finely chopped
 salt and pepper

Grate the cucumber and place it in a sieve over a large bowl. Salt the cucumber and mix it around. Leave it for 30 minutes to 2 hours, occasionally pressing the cucumber gently into the sieve to get the liquid out. The salt will help leach the water out of the cucumber.

Line another sieve (or the same one, cleaned) with paper towel or cheesecloth and pour the yogurt into it. You can leave it for as little as 1 hour on the counter or overnight in the fridge. The longer you leave it, the thicker it will get. This is how Greek yogurt is made!

Mix the strained cucumber with the yogurt and the other ingredients, then taste. Adjust the salt and pepper and add any more dill or onion.

Enjoy on sandwiches, as a dip, with pita or tortilla chips, or over meatballs, kebabs or anything spicy.

So many of the recipes in this collection can be easily modified to your taste. Learning to cook with different spices, herbs, and aromatics will instantly elevate your cooking and open up new and interesting possibilities.

Spices are expensive to buy, but since you use such small amounts, they end up costing pennies per recipe. If you're able to shop around, look for inexpensive spices in bulk at ethnic markets.

Below, I've ranked what I feel are the most important seasonings, but if you already know what you like, please listen to yourself! I know that my sister would rank chipotle powder just under salt, so do as your heart commands.

CHILI FLAKES: Chili is a great choice if you like things a little spicy. I add just a dash of chili flakes to almost all savory dishes to give them a little more dimension. Plus, chili flakes are usually pretty cheap.

CUMIN OR CUMIN SEEDS: Cumin goes well with so many flavors, and is essential in Mexican and Indian cuisine.

CURRY POWDER: Curry powder is a bunch of south Asian spices blended together. I prefer to make my own out of individual spices, but if you're new to curry, consider buying a blend to start out. If you love it, start buying the separate spices.

DRIED OREGANO AND DRIED THYME: Both of these herbs are still tasty when dried. They add a lot of flavor to chili, soups, or roasted vegetables. However, don't bother with dried basil, dried cilantro, or dried dill unless you particularly like them and can't afford to get them fresh. They lose almost all their magic when dried.

CINNAMON: This is probably everyone's favorite "sweet" spice. If you like baking, get some as soon as possible.

PAPRIKA AND SMOKED PAPRIKA: Paprika adds a bit of heat, although not nearly as much as chili flakes. Instead, it gives you a great mild pepper taste. Smoked paprika is my favorite way to get smoky flavors into a dish. These are by no means essential, but they're lots of fun.

Spices and Aromatics

Try the flavor combinations below on anything from rice to roasted chicken to vegetables. Mix them into butter, or add them to popcorn, toast, or vegetables. In short, experiment!

lemon zest and garlic
oregano, cumin, and chili powder
cumin seeds, coriander seeds, and mustard seeds
onion, garlic, and ginger
anchovy, garlic, and chili
salt, pepper, and Romano or Parmesan
onion, chili, and fresh cilantro
sage, rosemary, and thyme
lemon, olives, and garlic
chipotle powder and lime
pickling spices
paprika and fresh dill
garlic and fresh parsley
fennel seeds and fresh parsley
orange, lemon, and lime zest
ginger, cinnamon, and black pepper
cardamom, coriander, and bay leaf
coconut, chili, and lime
scallions and fresh cilantro
garlic and fresh basil

Thanks

This book was made possible by the more than 5,600 generous people who supported my Kickstarter campaign. These fine folks donated more than 8,000 free printed copies of the book for individuals and families who needed them, and helped me offer tens of thousands of copies to non-profits at near cost. Those supporters who wanted to be named appear below. To each of them—and the thousands more who remain anonymous—my deepest thanks.

_elmer -jgw- "Huck" the dog @dontcallmecosmo @doodie @kcunning @nt1 @roasterjoe @sonicdeath ~Johno =) 5 Angries 78 Tarot A Canadian family A couple of poor food enthusiasts A former single mom on food stamps who pulled through and made a better life for herself, you can too! A good Christian A Kickstarter A lotus blossom and justice for all A Sheuerman A Wells A. Ojinaga A.J. Mullins A.O Aakash Mehendale Aarni Koskela Aaron Greenberg Aaron Kent Aaron Luk Aaron R. Sturm Aaron Rainey-Spence Aaron Shelley Abbie Read Abby Abby Horstmann Abdilatif Mohamud Abigail Blum Abigail Pope acab Adam Christopher Bryant Adam Griffin Adam Helgeson Adam J. Netzel Adam Kafka Adam Mann Adam Scicchitano Adam White Adam Wong Adele Schatschneider Adeline Yurovsky Adomas Paltanavicius Adrian Tache Adriane Ruzak Adrianne Cology Adrienne Stortz Adrish Hussain Aeble Business Services Inc. Afton Tyree Agata Williams Agathe Aggelakis Agnes Wagenhäuser Agnieszka Pienczykowska Agos Aimee Lavers Aimee Owen Aimee Smith Aivis Silins Ajit K. Gujrati Alan Alan Aquino Alan C Miller Alan Kennedy Alan Millard Alanna Simone Alayna Nestman Alberto Farinello Alberto Garnelo Alec Megginson Alejandro Jose Parjus Alek and Wendy Dembowski Alessandro Bottin Alex Abboud Alex and Naomi Alex B Alex Basalyga Alex Benjamin Alex Boerstler Alex Caton Alex Dres Alex Hodgson Alex King Alex Klein Alex L Alex P Alex Siguenza Alex Thrailkill Alex Tittiger Alexa Hirsch Alexander Ayer Alexander Ebin Alexander Panzeri Alexander Plath Alexander Roessner Alexander the Drake Alexander Y. Hawson Alexey Tyurin Alexis Carpenter Alfie Tham Ali Latorre Alice Griffin Alice Gyllenkrok Alice Tobin Alicia Elliott Alicia McDonnell Alison Quinn Alison Rigazio Alison Seligson Alissa B. Levy Alissa Conaty Alistair Mackay Alistair, Cathryn, and Leah Windsor Allan Hone Allen Allen Berrebbi Allen Schmidt Allison Lyttle Allison Nguyen Allison Salmon Allison Thomson-Vicuna Allison, Chris, and Ben Gallaway Allon Yosha Allyson Martin Almar Sheikh alysha naples Alyssa Anne Morrell Alyssa Bostian Alyssa Gustwiller Amanda and Ian Smith Amanda Arthur-Struss Amanda Baronowski Amanda Bee Amanda Farough Amanda Flake Amanda Fuller Amanda Hagg Amanda Hale-Williams Amanda Helstrom and Curtis Whitecarroll Amanda Kaczmarek Amanda Kirshner Amanda Leonard Amanda Nelis Amanda Page Amanda Potter Cole Amanda St.Germain Amanda Young Amarjot Singh Amber Amber and Zach Berninger Amber Leedham Amber McKenzie Amber Poston Amber Simpson Amber Watson Ambrosia Kingstone Ame Kaplan Amelia J. Alba Amelia Shister amena ahmad Amerite Ami Bhatt and Arun Nagarajan Amin Ghafelehbashi Amrita Singh AMS16 Amy Bentley Amy Beshara Amy Brande Amy Eisenberg Amy Glass Wellness Amy Heckel Amy Lynn Amy Oberholtzet Amy Osekowsky Amy Perez Amy Plummer Amy Pombo Amy S. Amy Schultz Amy Shah Amy Shelden Amy Thompto Amy Viehweg Amy W Amy Westphal Amy Wilhelm Amy Wilson Amy Yao Ana Byrne Ana McGrath Anastasia H Anastasia Melekou André Sabosch Andrea Arrasmith Andrea Baca Andrea Chan Andrea Charest Andrea Clara Augustin Andrea Imperatori Andrea M. Mucci Andrea Sciamanna Andrea Sletten Andreas Moraitis Andreas Olsson Andreas Wiederkehr Andreea Bostan Andrew Andrew Grosenbach Andrew Humphrey Andrew Kwon Andrew Matteson Andrew Nuckols Andrew Pollock Andrew Porter Andrew Sim_saiD Dodge Andrew Smith Andy Duong Andy Hoeschele Andy R Andy Schultz Andy Warwick Andy, Jennifer, and Milo Peters Angel Hill Angel Stachnik Angela Chatha Angela Floyd Angela Martinez Angela Nguyen-Dinh Angela Yen Angela York Crane Angelica Jusino Angey Wilson Angie Doan Angie Reiber Anh H. Nguyen Anh-Tu Nguyen Anita Brearton Anita DiBlasi Anita Knight Anita Marie Griffin, @OrganicExpert Anita Wilson Anja Valdes-Cuprill Anjan Ann C. Pagel Ann Fitzpatrick Ann Kinney Ann Marie Lund Ann Mott Ann Muth Ann Rox Anna Bradley Anna Citak Anna Deem Anna Donnell Anna Ellis Anna golden Anna McDuff Anna Rodriguez Anna Tibbetts Anna Watson Carl Anna-Katharina Becker Anne Anne Hogan, Rebel Milk Anne Miller Anne Nesse Anne O'Hehir Annette S Annette Slonim annie cakes Annie Carlon Annie Coyne Annie Terracina Annie Wall Annie Wildey

Anonymous person who believes giving, even a small amount, is good for the soul anthony biello Anthony Collins Anthony Edwards and Nadia Haniff-Edwards Anthony Lancaster Anthony M. Munoz Anthony McDougle antiphrastic Anton Shageyev Antonio Vega-Pacheco Anu French Anup and Rina Patel Anya Adams Anya Colón Appdaddy April Allen April Barreiro April Katherine April Maxey April Slocum Apryl Dailey Archie McLean Ardon Taylor Ari-Pekka Hirsimäki Ariel Leong Arielle Hurst Arielle Pinzon Bates Aries Chau Chi Kwong Arjun Arlyn Davich Arnav Shah Arnold Pronto Aroldo de Rienzo III Art Mezins Artemis Clydefrog ArtNYC Artur Jonczyk Ash, Hampshire, England Ashish Kumar Ashlee Bennett Ashley Brooke Toussant Ashley Casovan Ashley Duncan Ashley Marie Thompson Ashley Raethel Ashley Spivak c/o Alyson Spivak Ashley Turner Ashley Wagner Ashley Williams Ask la Cour Rasmussen Astro Lark Atomic City Roller Girls Audrey Hopkins Audrey Mackey Aunt Sheila and Uncle Bill Austen Tate Austin Warawa Autumn Bea Autumn Hahn Aviv Tomer Awesome Emily Harris Awkward Hug Azariah, Deven, Madeleine, and Evelyn Stevens Azlina Thoen Azoz158 B Beaver B. Vande Kolk Baer Charlton Bailey de Iongh Barb McDermott Barbara Baillargeon Barbara Hartmann Barbara Knaster Barbara Mosley Barbara Nock Barbara Opyt Barbara Shore Barry Strugatz Barton L. beaglemama Beatrice Copeland Beau Brossman Becca Fraser Becca Schall Becca Trachtenberg Beci Russell becki Becky Altmann, CWPC Becky and Carsten Mundt Becky and Charley Becky Decker Becky Morrette Becky Simkins Bedac beentsy belinda chin Belinda Conn Belinda Lee Bella E. Ben and Jackie Landes Ben and Katie Mallory Ben Chapman Ben Daeuber Ben Esau Ben Gelinas Ben H Ben Killorin Ben M Ben Potrykus ben torrens Ben Zerante Bend Kung Fu Bendyburn Benj Binks Benjamin A. Phipps Benjamin Binninger Benjamin James Ethelred Bartlett Hanbury-Aggs Benjamin Keele Bennett Beutel Berek Marcus Bertrand Garbassi betabrain Beth Allan Beth Georgian Beth Kirkpatrick Beth Lacey Gill Beth Morton Beth Mueller Beth Ptalis Hough Beth Segers Beth Sheldon Bethany Bethany O'Neill and Jason Sanchez Bethany Stolle Bethel Nathan Betsy Duncan Betsy Kusenberg Betsy Maixner Betsy VanLeit Better Living By Choice Bettina Thompson Betty Garcia Beverley Markowitz Beverley Scherdin Beverly Ramsey Bez Straz Bianca Bockman Bianca Goo Bill Graham Bill Jefferson Bill Noble and Desiree Storch Bill Wiswesser Bill Woodcock and Audrey Plonk BillBil Bitter Root Cultural Heritage Trust BJ Beyersbergen bk Blair Harley Blumenkati BNF Bob Selim Bob Waltenspiel Bobbi H. Bobbie Nichols Bodo Kittler Bonbon Melius Bonnie Bishop Bonnie L. Gray Bonnie Raymond Bonnie Watts Bonnie Wilson Boris Hampp Borja Huertas Boyd Mitchell Brad and Kristy Cronkrite Brad Boettcher Brad Corwin Brad Dougherty Brad Lee Brad Scanlan Brad Zehr Branden Miller Brandi Iryshe Brandi L. Fulk Brandi Thompson, RD, LD/N Brandon and Heather Thomas Brandon Millwood Brandon Webber Branka Tokic Mangala Bre Gallagher Brekke family Brenda Boston Brenda Head Brendan Brendan Brown BrennaK Brennan and Alexis Crellin Brennan and Julie Gerle Brent A. Middleton Brent Neil Bret Farber Brett Barker Brett Heeger Brett Jones Brett, Michelle, and Avery Johnson Brian Alenduff Brian and Donna Kearney Brian Anderson Brian Connery Brian Enigma Brian Eugenio Herrera Brian Fox Brian Hart Brian Kowal Brian L. Curtis Brian McAdam Brian R McDermott Brian Resnevic Brian Santistevan Brian Sierkowski Brian Stein Brian Trotter Brian White Brian Zielinski Brian Zuber Briana Rindfleisch Brianna Garcia Brianne D. Brice Grunert Bridget A Brownell Bridget Gannon Bridget K. Bridget Lydon Bridget Maniaci Briggs Britney Britt Quinan Britt Rodriguez Britt Wright Brittany and Mark Brittany Douglas Hunt Brittany Ellis Brittany Janis Brittney Le Blanc Brooke and Nate Eliazar-Macke Brooke Bell Brooke Estin Bruce Davey Bruce Venne Bruno Beildeck Bry-Ann Yates Bryan Bryan Calo and Trish Partch Bryan Dixon Bryan Dreiling Bryan Huang D Bryan J Wlas Bryan Jordan Bryan Ting Bryce Boltjes Brynn Palmer Buck Goggin Butter and Scotch Butter Music And Sound buzzedhoneys.com, raw urban honey C Rosser C. Laville C. Mosher C. Stives C.L. O'Byrne c.o.d. Cahlo Re Moon Caileigh Rhind and Phil Wortman Cait Cusack Caitlin A. Caitlin Gabelmann Caitlin Guzzo Caitlin Lantier, MS, RD, LD Cali Cally Thalman Calum W Calvin Chan Calvin He Cameron and Jennifer Hodges Cameron Beckmann Cameron J Larsen Camilla Crane Camilla Hammer Camille Reaves Campbell's Bakery Candace Uhlmeyer Candice Bailey Candra Murphy Canela Cara Kindig Caren Davidkhanian Carina Scheiberlich Carla Dawes Carla Hidalgo Carleton Torpin Carley Navratil Carlos Díez Carlos Medeiros Carlos Penner Carlos y Rene @ Casa PyP Carly and Michael Hackman Carly Campbell Carly Westling Carmen Carol Elaine Cyr Carol Lundergan Carol Sandin Cooley Carol Thorne Caroline Boice Caroline Ernst Caroline Kren Caroline Moore-Kochlacs Caroline Richards Carolyn and Wesley Buckwalter Carolyn Crippen Carolyn Lerbs Carolyn Z Carrie Dellesky and Dane Yocco Carrie Prudhomme Carrie Sedlak Carsten Kummerow Casey Greene Casey Harmon Casey Reeder Cassie and Nathaniel Cassie Grove Cassie M Wilson, Whole Body Wellness Practitioner Cassondra C. Cat Rigby Catherine Casillas Catherine Droser Catherine Riihimaki Catherine van Zanten Cathy Presper Cathy Williams Catie Leary Catie Murphy CDM Cecille Nguyen Cedric Jean-Marie Celene C. Celeste Ransom Cesar Loke Alvarez Chad Cleven Chad Homan Chad Puclowski Chad Rousseau Chad Smith CHANDA Chanda Unmack Chandler Bullion Chandra Magee Charlene Barina charlene mcbride Charles Irving Charles Letcher III Charles Ludeke Charles McNeely Charles Rivet Charles Vardeman Charles Zapata Charles Zuzak Charley Johnson, RN Charlie and Catie Lauria Charlie Seaman Charlotte Beaudet Charlotte Holmes Charmaine (kiyo) Liew Charmaine Fuller Chase Henderson Chase Montgomery Chef Carla Contreras Chef Kelli Mae Kelly Chelle Destefano Chelsea Clifton Chelsea Keena Chelsea McQuaid Chelsea Neblett Chely Córdova Chen Sharon Cheroot Cherry Street Farmers Market Cheryl Chiou Schall Cheryl Martin Cheryl, Tobi, and Rowan Ackerman Cheryll Kregear Cheyenne Kelly chez geller Chi Chi and Ju Ju Chiarello family Chien Yeh Jan Chiharu Ito Chloe Lines Chloe Rudd Chng Chin Joo Chow family Chris and Robyn Leitner Chris B. Chris Bacarella Chris Boutet Chris Fox Chris Hardham Chris Huynh Chris Jacobson Chris James Chris Jones Chris Knadler Chris Larson Chris M Chris Mattern Chris Neufeld Chris Newell Chris Olsen Chris Stier Chris Tam Chris Wilson Chris, Laura, Miranda, and Margaret Chrispey Christa and Johnny Eggz Christa Huntley Christian Franci Christian Fuchs Christian Guy Christian Yancey and Joe Yeaman Christina Demyen Christina Tannert Christine Devine Christine Favilla Christine Hyde Christine Marqua Christine R. Carmody Christoph Widmer, Switzerland Christopher Brumgard Christopher J Henderson Christopher Muzatko Christopher P. Christopher Thornhill Christopher Weeks Christyn Levy Chrystal and Chris Gualtieri, in memory of Karen Castle Chuck Vining Ciara Sanker Ciaran Davis-Wall Cindie Cindy Bradley Cindy Chuah Cindy Powers

Cindy Ternes Snydacker Cindy Thompson Streett Claire and Ed Bacher Claire Smither Wulsin
Clara Schuhmacher Clare Ferguson Claude Convers Claudia Nelson Clayton
clayton whetung Clemens Mezriczky Clevonne Jacobs Cliff and Toni Thompson Clio Tarazi
CMCastillo Coach Paul Cody McNeill Cody Perkins Coeli Colby Coleen Hackett
Colin HB Lee Colleen and Kim Colleen Clary and family Colleen McCormack-Maitland
Connie A. Ress Connie Cusick Connie Phillips Connor Joseph Smith Conrad Shen
Constantine Kousoulis Cooperative Press Cora Anderson Cora Neil coral Cord Patrick
Corey and Shirley Mouer Corey L. Cori Chavez Cori May CorwinWoody Cory Dieterich
Cory Dillon Cory Vandenberghe Cosanna Preston-Idedia and Lucky Idedia Courtney Antonioli
Courtney Rittinger Courtney Shea Owen Courtney Shuster Craig Fausnacht Craig Handley
Craig McNaughton Crapnurse Cristendra Cristina Dominguez-Eshelman Cristy Spottswood
Cristy Troia Crystal Chitwood Crystal Gammon Crystal Kerr Crystal R Van Wieren
Curt Buckley Curtis Curtis and Heather Curtis Hirabayashi Cygnus Rockwood Cynthia
Cynthia Disbrow D C Schumacher D J Althaus D W Yarbrough D. Clarke Evans D. Dial
D. Marie DaHill Dailey family Dale R. Dale Rose Damian Barnes Damian Pieries
Damien Kluczinske Damit Senanayake Damon and Marge Anderson Dan and Elizabeth Conley
Dan and Jane Iehl Dan Fishgold Dan Ford Dan Lazin Dan Napierski Dan Nielsen
Dan Partington Dan R Dan Ratner Dan Tea and Amy-Jo Russ Dan-Tam Pham Dana
Dana Aspinwall Dana Buske Dana Cameron Dana Chahidi Dana Freeman Dana Rae
Dang Griffith Dani L Pruitt Danica Sergison Daniel Daniel and Lillian Mahaney
Daniel Dickerman Daniel E. Harlow Daniel Freytes Daniel Head Daniel Kaszor
Daniel O'Connell Daniel Philippe Daniel R. Leonard Daniel Rinehart Daniel Santoso
Danielle Dugan Danielle Holbein Danielle Peña Danielle Roberts Danny and Lizzie Varner
Danny and Stephanie Lee Danny Das Neves Danny Mendoza Daphne Horton Darcy L
Darin Vermillion Darker Days Radio Darline Heck Darren Hansen Darryl Newberry
Dashmeet Singh Dave and Jill Dave Ballard Dave Banno Dave Burtman Dave Cournoyer
Dave Haylett Dave Lawson Dave LeCompte Dave Marsh Dave McDonald Dave Violago
Dave West David and Anita Schamber David and Elizabeth Sims David and Jozette Papa
David and Katie Buys David and Sonya Reiland David B Moore David Blessing david bradley
David Cheung David Drexler David Gallaher David Hilder David Hooper David J. D.
David J. Paul David Lawson David Lazarus David McKane David Miller David Moghaddam
David Plater David Pond David Rhodes David Rinaldi Jr. David Ruby David S. Lord
David Sarpal David Scannell David Schultz David Souther and Annie Levine David Tomashek
David W. Weaver David Weinman David Wright Dawn Benish Dawn Louis-Jean
Dawn M. Janz Dawn Oshima Dawn Tarpey Dawne Jeffreys Dayzen Weks VII DBT
Dé-zér Khandro Dean Housden Dean Pironi Deanna Lagace Deanna Penney deb
Deb Miner Debbie Goble Deborah Ingram Deborah Iquique Deborah L Wheeler
Deborah Svenson Deborah Trevithick Debra P. Debra's Natural Gourmet Defiantly Healthy
Deirdre McCarthy Delia Gable Delia M. Rivera-Hernandez Delia Macias della Denise Blatnik
Denise Eicher Denise Riley Derek Derek Crawford Derek Kwan Derek Pollard Derek Y.
Dethe Elza Devin R Bruce Devon K. Devon Peters Dexie Llenado Diana Jensen Diana Lu
Diana Lynn Small Diana Lynne Rochon Diane Freaney Diane Le Diane Lee Diane Sparks-
Justice Dietmar Dilan Leon Dinah Dinah Sanders dinkyshop.com Dinyar
Dirk "diggler" Davie Dirk Huygelen Djimon Hounsou Dmitry Igumnov Doc Hobbes
Dominic Sabatier Dominique Holzer Dominique Navarro Don McNeil Don Quach
Donald Darnell Donna Barnes Donna Giles Donna Gordon Donna H Donna Manalo
Donna Peebles Donny Tsang Dorian Nasby Dorian Sanders Dorota Was Dorothy Ng
Dorte Sheikh Dotan Dvir Doug Doug Creek Doug Ittner Douglas Dollars Dr. Julius Buski
Dr. Rachel McKinnon Dr. Shelby Worts Dragan Colakovic Drew Geen
Drs. Scott Moats and Michele Moul Duane and Paula Fults Dub Dunlevy Dustin
Dustin W. Cammack Dwest Dwight Bishop Dylan Crowley Dylan Forest Dylin Martin
Dylon E.J. Cronin E.J. Johnston Eagertolearn Ean Behr Ebo Dawson-Andoh Ed
Ed and Chris Black Eddy Wang Edith Finley Edna Ann Rouse Eduardo Câmara
Edward Bennett Edward Chik Edward Goggin Edward Heavrin Edward LeBlanc
Edwyn Tiong Eeshwar Rajagopalan ef-pe.at egg and yolk Ehtesh Choudhury
Eileen and Dave Morrison Eileen LaBoone Eileene Coscolluela EK Becker and CS Chugh
Elaine Blank Elaine Block Elaine M. King Elaine Marshall Elaine Zuo Eleanor Watkins
Elena A. Becker Elena Von Essen Eli Sotos Elisabeth and Michael Elliot Elise D. Evans
Elise Nussbaum Elisha Roberts Elisse Lorenc Eliza Elmer Elizabeth and Kristen McIntire
Elizabeth Bridges Elizabeth Dale Elizabeth Hunter Elizabeth Jablonski Elizabeth Johnston
Elizabeth K. Elizabeth Kenyon Elizabeth Mieke Elizabeth Miner, Thrive This Day
Elizabeth Mukherjee Elizabeth Neeld Elizabeth Q Davis Elizabeth Ross Falk Elizabeth Schroder
Elizabeth Tudhope Elizabeth Williams Ellen Power Ellen Schmidt Ellen Shapiro
Ellen Solomon Elli Fragkaki Elliott M. Elliott Rajnovic Elrod family Elyssa Lind
EM and Mike Rodewald Emerald Watters Emeth Hesed Emil Hemdal Emily
Emily and Dan Berriochoa Emily Beth Emily Brown Emily Crovella Emily Griffin
Emily Gruen Emily Heist Moss Emily Leathers Emily Mitchell Emily Schienvar Emily Ties
Emily Vanston Emily Walter Emily Zarr Emma Boley Emma Gardiner Emma Rose and Lili
Emmanuel Jose Emry and Olivier Stam Enrico Phillis Enrique Piedrafita
Eri Kawakami and Andrés del Valle Eric and Lindsay MacCallum Eric and Noelle Braun
Eric Brodie Eric Foster Eric Hensley Kron Eric Klipp Eric Koleda Eric Storm Eric Welsby
Eric Wolf Erica Agran Erica Dee Erica Garcia Erica Parker Erica Peters Erica Templeman
Erick Aubin Erik Kearney Erika Hille and Remon Eltaii Erika R. Cerda Erika Thorkelson
Erin Bourne Erin Cullinane Erin Dudley-Krizek Erin Gibbemeyer Erin Liman Erin McGann
Erin McLaughlin Erin Tiburcio Erin Whitney Fox Smith Ernesto Montoya Ernie Torres
Etchasketcher Ethan Landa Ethan Rainwater etherglow Eugenio Frias-Pardo Eurie Chung
Eva Eva Crawford Eva DePue Eva Townsend Evakay Favia Evan Farmer Evan P. Potman
Evan Prowten Evan Schaeffer Evelyn D. Everett Everleigh Ruschman Evie Ewan Lauchland
Ewan Moorfoot Faith Savill Falk von Boehn falldeaf Falling Sky Farms Family König Beatty
Family of Anna Ballinger famousgames.co Fan of good works Farmers Everywhere
Feda Hankic Fei-Ling Tseng Felicia Zimmerman Felix Felix K. Fen and Martin Burley
Fernando Mendoza-Alanis Filip Bul Krajník Filip De Pessemier, mindcoach.be
filmcrafter.com filmstory.org Finn Semmelink Finny Fiona Glover Firuzeh Fix Flo
Flor Maria Macias Florence Kitten Florence Payette Florian Hirt Florian Horsch Forderick
Foss Curtis Fran McCoy Francie Oblinger Francis Luk Frank Corey Frank M. Cannizzaro
Frank Olechnowicz Frank Robert Frank S Frannie Jones Fred Hapgood Fred Weber
Freda Eang Frederic Landes Fresh Start Foods Fung To O G S Candy G. Woods Gabby K
Gabi C Gabriel Proulx-Jalbert Gabriele Briggs Gabriella Stops Gaddy Gaia Willis
Gail Gibbs Gail Hernandez Gailann Lee Wagoner Gavin "halkeye" Mogan Gavin Smith
Geistlingers Gemma Critchley Generaal Genie Gratto Geoffrey and Sierra Miank
Geoffrey and Tanya Roth Geojus George and Karen Gibbs George B. Higgins George Campbell
George Edwards George H Golden George Read III George Young Georgy Melnikov
Geralyn Beers Gerben Z Geri Collecchia Gerzain Maldonado GG Crew Giacomo Zacchia
Gilson family Gina Clune Gina Colagioia Gina Dimino Gina Freeman Gina Lawrence
Gina Pensiero Gina Spengel Ginny Flasha ginny guzman Gitta de Vaan Giu Alonso
Giuseppe Rossi Gizmo and Gadget Gladys Nubla Glen Glen "the Bodarian" Bodor
Glen and Julia Ferguson Glenn Clatworthy Glenn Hitt Glenna Klaver Gloria and Dan Garrett
Gloria MacKinnon, @exohglo Gonzalez-Kinnebrew family Gonzalo Drinot and Sydney Herrin
Good and Cheap Grand Master Kathy Sand Cope Gopakumar Sethuraman Gordon
John Henry Wong/Dubs/Wonger/got wong? Grace Flinsch Grace Gilles Grace Lim Gradster
Graham Bakay Graham King Graham Knox Graham Marshall Grandma Patti
Grandpa Chair Grant Burkhardt Grant McLaughlin graventy Greg "Healthy Chef" Brandes & Dee
Greg Davies Greg Davis Greg Leach Greg McDougall Greg Mund Greg Shaffer
Greg, Shona, Sarah, Sasha, and Smudge Gregory Damiani Gregory Steenbeek Greta Frost
Gretchen Addi Gretchen and David Zalkind Gretchen Northrop Guadalupe Albuquerque
guardian J Guillermo Marshall Gus Gwen Golden Gyoo Sung Choi Gyroplast
H Lynnea Johnson H. Higa Hal Cantwell Halee Dinsey Allison Hamish weir
Hannah and Brody Hannah Brown Hannah Gardner Hannah Naomi Jamieson
Hannah Rothman Hannah Spiegelman Hans Hans Shejama Schmidt
Happy Tsugawa-Banta Harper Masino Harris Masters Harry Reutter Harvey Simmons
Hayden McAfee Heath and Dani Glasscock Heath Prewitt Heather Adler
Heather and Salim Cain Heather Beath Heather Bowen Heather D. McLean Heather Dyer
Heather Hewitt Chowdhury Heather Hintze Heather Hoyles Heather McGivney
Heather Snell Heather, Curtis, and Charlie Heidi Burch Heidi Kirkpatrick Heinrich Langos
Helen Sandoz Helena C. Yardley Helena Chestnut Henk-Jan
Hennepin County MN Nurse-Midwives Henning C-F Herman Hey Rooster General Store
hillary bergh Hillary Newell hilt-d Hiram's Mad Organist Hoa X. Nguyen
Hochiminh Rosario holli watts Holly Bartel Holly Colbourne Holly H. Archer Holly Hayes
Holly Peterson Hope Mueller Hope Pascoe HubuMedia Huddleston family Hudson
Hungry Harris Hunter Bennett-Daggett Hussein Sulaiman I Miller Iain Ilich
Ian Malinowski Ian Matthew Michael Burg Ian McCrowe Ian Sheh Ian Skibbe Ian Westcott
iarehui ICON Motion Pictures id8 Design Ida Walker Idia A Ikai Lan Imani J Dean
In honor of the Vermont Food Bank In memory of Carroll E. Selph In memory of Jennie Haydel
In memory of Nicholas Holt inspiremotion Ion Marqvardsen Irene I. Iris Polit Di Paola
Iris Tse Isaac M. Walker Isaiah Tanenbaum Ismaeel Razavi Iso Stein Iva Cheung
J David Baker J Gagnon J Papineau J. Meyer J. Quincy Sperber J. Rock J'aime Stratton
J&S Des Jaaq Jac Willis Jace Nay Jack Dalrymple, Cap And Cut, LLC Jack Fleming
Jack Hutchings Jacki Purtell Jackie Goulet and Susan Goulet Jackie Rosenfeld Jackson West
Jaclyn and Daniel Bernstein Jacob A Palmer Jacob Feutz Jacob Pauli Jacob Wisner
Jacqueline Windh Jacquelyn Piette Jacqui B. jade tree Jaewoo Kim Jag Jake Farrell
Jake Nichols Jake Rayson James and Karon Davis James Bauer James Chesky
James Delecki James DeMarco James H. Murphy Jr. james helton James Hess
James Husum James Leung James MacCarthy James Maxhimer James McCall
James Meehan James Rossiter and Katie Bonnar James Rybolt James Smith James V Reynolds
James Wilmot James Yuen James-Ross Harrison Jamie Antonisse Jamie Mrgich
Jamie Stelter Jamie Taylor jamie, tasmania Jamison Gray Jamison R. Monahan
Jan Martin Ahlers Jan Sepp Jane Jane Broumley Jane Colleen Hall Jane Cruice, RN
Jane Hanson Jane Jerardi Jane Lam Jane Metzger Jane Purvis Janell Regaldo Janelle E.
Janelle W Janet Janet Buchwald Janet Camille Hood Janet Williams Janette Rounds
Janey freid Janice Karpenick Janice Murphy Jarin Udom Jarrod Jarrod Lombardo
Jasmine Melanie April Kelly jasmine wolf Jason and Gina Rogers Jason Berry Jason Burrow
Jason Daugherty jason e. bean Jason Gifford Jason Hawes Jason Kapalka Jason Kenny
Jason Miller Jason Wells Jason Zan Jay Jay B Avitable Jay Graham Jay Kastner
Jay Ricciardi Jay Shah Jaye Buksbaum Jaymie Testa JBrien Cezar Barcoma JD Champagne
JD Reeves Jean Manz Jean Prijatel Jean-François Léger Jean-Sebastien Busque
Jeanie McAlpine Jeanne Bishop, America's Sensory Impaired Veterans Organization Jeanne W
Jeannine Emery Jeff and Jenna Jeff Clark Jeff Enlow Jeff Iseminger Jeff Jacobsen
Jeff Kapustka Jeff Lehman Jeff Lin Jeff Lininger Jeff Matsuya jeff parriott Jeff Tsai
Jeffery and Lydia Simpson jefflindt.com Jeffrey and Lori Simkowski Jeffrey Blank
Jeffrey J. Jett II Jen A. Jen Dadek Jen Hoscheid Jen Jamar, lifewithlevi.com Jen Lewin
Jenn de la Vega Jenn Dyno Jenna Weiler Jenni and Brian Bost Jennie Reinish
Jennifer and Samuel Soliman Jennifer Brunette Jennifer C. Moats Jennifer Capozzi
Jennifer Chang Jennifer Cloud Jennifer Coulter Jennifer Dyson Jennifer E.D. Hahn
Jennifer Essler Jennifer Jackson Jennifer Jakes Jennifer Jelliff-Russell Jennifer Jusinski
Jennifer K. Jennifer Kirkgaard Jennifer Konikowski Jennifer L. Sarnowski Jennifer McInnis
Jennifer Moore Jennifer Murphy Jennifer Norton Jennifer Palm Jennifer Peepas
Jennifer Pomeranz Jennifer Read Jennifer Schiff Berg Jennifer Shackelford Jennifer Skytt
Jennifer Strauss Gurss Jennifer Tuttle Jennifer Wilkinson Jennifer Wylie Jenny Blakeney
Jenny Lasley Jenny Mudge Jenny Vaughn Jens Anders Bakke Jens Dehlke
Jeramy Zimmerman Jeremiah and Shannon Tuhn Jeremy and Leslie Miller Jeremy Canfield
Jeremy M Jerika Teare Jess Blinn Jess Mott Wickstrom Jessa Anderson Jesse F.
Jesse Inoncillo Jesse Lansner and Elizabeth Call Jesse Michael Jessica A. Walsh Jessica Allred
Jessica and Josh Warren Jessica Bader Jessica Berglund Jessica Cole Jessica Del Vecchio
Jessica Gallagher Jessica Graham Jessica Greene Jessica Jensen Jessica Jones Jessica Koga
Jessica Kral Jessica McCartney Jessica P. Tharp Jessica Riga Jessie Glover Boettcher
Jessie Tang Jessy Singh Jesus Bautista Jesus C. Duran JET JGRS Barnes Jhenifer Pabillano
Jia Guo Jibby Varghese Jill Bucaro Jill D'Alessandro and family Jill Jungheim
Jim and Kris jim bayerle Jim Boney Jim Cosmano Jim Fennell Jim Gill Jim Phillips
Jim Rutkowski Jr. JJ Sommerville JLC Jo Anne Jo Gill Joachim W. Walewski Joan Baggs
Joan Cockell Joan Johnson Joan Schumaker joane farrell Joanna Alario Joanna Ranelli
Joanne Chayut Joanne Rosario Joanne Y Jocke Axelsson Jodi Shipley Jody Knapke
Jody Veith Joe and Alison Kornbrodt Joe and Robin Birdwell Joe Ballou Joe Beason
Joe Bernard Joe Carter Joe Gonwa Joe H. Joe Hsu, @jhsu Joe Nachison Joe Posner
joe rhodes Joe Spradley Joel Neely Joel Schachter Joel Suplido Joel Voelz Joerg Fricke
Johan Carlsson Johanna Wilson Johannes Robbins John A Connor John and Deb
John C Halcomb John Cascarano John Chappell John Christian Bethell John Colagioia
John Colburn John Darragh John Ferguson John Garcia John Giles John Heltsley
John J. Walsh IV John J. Williams John Jenkins Jr. John Leonardo Contarino John Mondin
John Pushnik John Rampton John Repass John Rieping John W Watson
John Wm. Thompson John, Michelle, and Morgan G Johnathan Salter Johnny Le

Johnny Wu Jon Jon Guy Jon Hovland Jonah and Brittany Gregory Jonathan Anders
Jonathan Chamberlin Jonathan D.M Jonathan gregory Jonathan Grothe Jonathan Harmon
Jonathan Hironaga Jonathan Landry Jonathan M. Broussard Jonathan Ostrowsky Joop
Jordan and Amanda Jordan and Eileen Park Peed Jordan Majeau Jordan McGary
Jorge Cocina Jose Angel Lara José L. Valiente José López Jose Sanchez II Joseph Daniels
Joseph Lockridge Joseph Mandrell Joseph Raff Joseph Watson-MacKay Josh Abramsohn
Josh and Laurie Barton Josh Baugher Josh Catone Josh Durairaj Josh Kjenner Josh Lobo
Joshua Goodwin Joshua Jabbour Joshua M. Diaz Joshua Shanks and Heather Barnett
Joshua Straub Joshua Wheaton Joy Zserai Joyia and Thom Jozel Bennet
Juan Pablo Ahues-Vasquez judders Jude and Woolf Kanter Judith Judith Harris
Judith Redding judith smyser Judy D Shelton Judy Dub Judy Frumkin JudyAnne Hutchison
Jufo Gold Association Juhis the Nuhis Juli-Ann Williams Julia Brucker Julia Clark
Julia Clayton Julia Johnsen Julia Perilli Julian and Jack Clark Julian Parr
Julie "Cannibal Rose" Thielen Julie Burt Pack Julie Dillon Julie Gerush Julie Hannon
Julie Lee Julie Rickert Julie Smith Julie Wolkoff Julien Fruchier
June Samadi and Brandon Holmes June Trizzino Junko Saito Jurgens B Jussi Hölttä
Justin Acosta Justin and Anne Swanson Justin Daues Justin Feller Justin M. Czerniak
Justin Myers Justin Phan Justin Roth Justin Tabibian Justine Henonin K Kanno
K. D. Bryan K.A. Farb Kaelynn Alykasa Laefon kaiser sosa Kaitlin Murphy Kaitlyn MacLeod
Kalyan Reddy Kamaria Kuhn Kanchana Fernando and Craig Kallal Kara Styles Karan S
Karel de Mooij Karen Karen and Lance Jones Karen Ann Bullock Karen Clark Karen Funseth
Karen Hess Karen Liebel Karen MacLaughlin Karen McKeown Karen Pekarcik
Karen Salsbury Karen Slagle Karen Ullman Karen Walsh Karen, Bellingham WA Kari L.
Kari M. Karie Fahrenholz Karin Fuerst Karina Manarin Karina Spencer Karis Blume
Karissa Karl and Erin Schulz Karl Schmidt Karl von Muller Karl-Olof "Kakan" Larsson
Karla Anker Karsten Holland Karyn Parks Kasserine Ross-Sheppard Kassidy Kanter
Kat Lapelosa Kate Kate Adamick, co-founder, Cook for America Kate and Greg Griffin
Kate Ashie Kate Bauer Kate H. Wilson Kate MacGregor Kate Mileur Kate O'Connell-Faust
Kate Peltz Kate Rossiter Kate Seiler Kate Whalen Kathe Falzer Katherine and Andrew Weber
Katherine Burns Katherine Cesario Katherine Krauland Katherine Moore Wines
Katherine Potter Katherine Romans Katherine Tulley Kathleen Conlogue Kathleen Dawson
Kathleen Gadway Kathleen Kitto and Dennis Waller Kathleen M. Herring Kathleen Smith
Kathleen T. Hanrahan Kathryn Mackenzie Kathryn McCauley Kathryn Rice
Kathy and Michael Elliott Kathy Jolly Kathy Komoll Kathy Lawrence
Kathy Nelson-Williams Kathy Nguyen Kathy Shannon and Matt Frank Kathy Waxler
Kathy Wicks Katie Goodrich Katie Jones Katie M. Katie McElroy Katie McGill
Katie Rangel Katie Shay Katie Shea Katie Shields Katie Stoyka Katie Wang Katie Watson
katofrafters Katrina Gwinn Katrina Rittershofer Kavanagh family Kavitha Ritesh Gudla
Kay M Cadena Kaydee Kreitlow Kayla Blyman Kayla Forshey Kayleigh Simmons
Kaylyn S. Gootman Keally Cieslik Keena Keith Warner Keladry Midlan Keldren
Kelli Currie Kelli Neier Kelly Kelly Ann Kelly Kelly Burns Gallagher Kelly Cole Kelly Goff
Kelly McClung Kelly Murray Kelly Schrank Kelly Stacy KellyS Kelsey Kitch Ken Allgood
Ken Chen Ken Cooper Ken Hoff Ken Klein Ken Nikolai Kendel Shore Kendra Lockman
Kendra Peters Kenette Louis Kenley Sturdivant-Wilson Kenneth E. Baker Kenny K.
Kent Kristensen Kernbanks Kerri Larkin Kerri Swail-Born Kerry Duncan Barnsley
Kerry Osborne Kevin and Shannon Grigsby Kevin Ascott Kevin C Huang Kevin Chow
Kevin FitzGerald Kevin Gawthrope Kevin Hofer and Laurie Zellmer Kevin J Schaeffer II
Kevin Jarvis Kevin L. Reevers Kevin Lee Kevin Matthew Murphy Kevin McClintock
Kevin Miller Kevin O'Connell Kevin Stilwell Kevin Wood Kieran O'Sullivan Kiki Anderson
Kim Kessler Kim Ketterer Kim Pasciuto-Wood Kim Wong Kimberly
Kimberly and Tyson Kroeger Kimberly Fine Kimberly Gibson Kimberly Muñoz Kimlee Smith
Kira Kefer kirk Kirk Stewart Kirsten Hurlburt Kirsti A. Dyer, HealthfulMD Kirsti Johanson
Kirsty Win Kitchen Overlord Kitty Y. Kiyana Santos Daba KJ Bosch Klara
KMunke Master Chef KN Chin-Griffin Knobby Horseman Knut Roger Strøm
Koen Vingerhoets Koko Kawasaki koroshiya Kourtney Robinson Kraken Maiden
Kris Berezanski Kris Burgess Kris Cabanas Kris Covlin Krista Benson Kristel England
Kristen Coatney Kristen Coty-Noel Kristen Farley Kristen Miller Abraham Kristen Schnelle
Kristen Vieson Kristen W. Kristen Wong Kristen, Estella, and Joel McClosky Kristi Howell
Kristi Ketchum Kristin Corona Kristin Hadfield Kristin Justice and Zachary Miller
kristina apodaca Kristina Hon Kristina Kaw Kristina Maude Hill Kristina Pisegna
Kristopher and Savannah Hall Kristopher Hoover Kristopher Theilen Kristy-Ann MacPherson
Kristyn Krystelle Robeniol KSENiA Kunal Ghevaria Kurt Anderson Kurt Mansperger
Kurtis Story Kyle and Kayla Williams Kyle Higgins Kyle McCormick Kyle Walker
Kyle White Kylie O'Neill-Mullin Kym Frankovelgia Kyra C. Kyriienko family
L. Madatovian L'ALTRO Design Lacey and Andi Losh Lachlan Berry Lady Chiviona
LadyAna Lainie W. Lakeysha Jones Lance425 Langh Kap Tuang Lara B. Lara Dossett
Larissa Barry Larissa Rüdiger Larissa Yu Laura laura asmussen Laura Baggs Laura Biddle
Laura Coelho Laura Corcoran Laura Daigle Laura Devin Laura E Strong Laura Friederich
Laura Gray Laura Jones Laura Klotz Laura Lee Franks Laura M Brown Laura Mae
Laura Musich Laura N Morgan Laura Niwa Laura O'Donnell Laura O'Quin Laura Patti
Laura Rodríguez Laura Snider Laura Suprock Laura Thomas Laurel Bobzien Laurel S
Lauren "The Librarian" Bryant Lauren and Greg Bixby Lauren Bloomenthal Lauren Egge
Lauren Eggert-Crowe Lauren Heacker Lauren Karp Lauren Leslie Lauren Patti
Lauren Reynolds Lauren Scanlan Lauren Shipp Lauren Vardaman Lauren Wittenberger
Lauri Dahl Laurinda Pudlo LaVerne Tolmie LCG Le Chef N5SQA Leah and Brian Eden
Leah Collins Leah Hochberg Leah Weatherspoon Leanne Fong LearningLab LA
Lee and Jessica Beacham Lee Burgess Lee Symes LeeAnn Maxwell Leif Hunneman
Leigh Anne Vanhoozer Leigh Johnston Lekisha Laster Lenora Polk Leona Peterson, L.M.S.W.
Leonard and Zepporah Magnan Leonard Lin Leong Yin Yin Leonides M. Leora Falk
Leron Culbreath Leshia-Aimée Doucet Lesley Dx leslie barkley Leslie Goldblatt Leslie Jordan
Leslie Maddock Leslie Poyzer Leslie Seltzer Leslie Walton, Earth Biscuit Foods Lexa Dundore
Lexu Leyanne Li Wang Liam and Theo Rich Liam Wilkinson Liana Lehua Lianne Longdo
Libby, Cici, and Ike Perella Liew Wee San Lil Copan Lil M. Liliana Troy Lillian Johnson
Lin McCormick Linda Alexander Linda and Chris LaBarre Linda Crawley Linda DeAngelo
Linda J Hewitt linda melsted Linda P. Nguyen Linda Parker Linda Saroeun
Linda Seagraves-haloi Linda Telkowski Linda, Robert, and Lily O'Neill Lindsay Hills
Lindsay Monser Lindsay Winter Lindsey Haskins Lindsey Wheeler Lindsey Wicks Lisa
Lisa Akiyama Lisa Barmby-Spence Lisa Behnke Lisa Benjamin Lisa Challender Lisa Conn
Lisa Cox Lisa Duffy Lisa Forsyth Lisa Hagen Lisa Hirsch Lisa Holmes Lisa Kilmartin
Lisa Partridge Lisa Paton Lisa Plotnik Lisa Raphael Lisa Ray Lisa Taylor Lisa Toro

Lisa W. Lisa Woodman Lisa7 Lissa Capo LIVID Liyana Winchell Liz and Mark Wilton
Liz and Robin Baker Liz Blasingame Liz Gerber Liz McAnder Liz Pienkos Liza Hall
Lizzie Taishoff Sweigart locallunatic Loenis and Kevin Logan "Logie" James
Logan and Alvina Mardhani-Bayne Lois Strand Lola DeBrosse Lomig Lorenz
Lorenz Kaspar Müller Loretta Permutt Lori Lori Conrad Lori Laney Lori Mastronardi
Lorien Green Lorraine La Pointe Louie Louis A. Tillman Louise Hall Louise Keamy
Louise Wasilewski Louise Williams Lourdes Iglesias Love Lovely Cakes Lovey Reynolds
LRA LubDub Foundation Luc Wilson Lucas Roven Luciano Sgarbi lucy hunnicutt
Luisa Alberto Luka Negoita Luke Coomes Luke Dacey Luke David Johnson Luke Knight
Luke M Stevens Luke Rutherford Lulu Kaye Luther Pearson Lydia Lydia J
Lydia Katsamberis Lydia Pegus Lyn Ignatowski Lynn Adler Lynn Barbato Lynn Brice Rosen
Lynn Casper Lynn Foster Lynn Hougle Lynn Knight Lynn Rudd Lynne Donnelly
Lynne Lightowler Lynne Sims Lyth Alobiedat M A Chiulli M L Faison M. Dawn King
M. S. Barger Maarten and Robert MAAZIK Mab Maci Peterson Maciek Maddie Kershow
Maddisun Barrows Maddy Kamalay Madeline Boyer Madeline Edmonds Madison Smite
Maegan Williams Maeve McLoughlin Magenta and Harrison Starbuck Maggie Murphy
Maggie Todd maggie valdespino Maida Spohrer Makshya Tolbert Malcolm Woade
Malgorzata Nishio Malissa and Ragan Mambo mamojo mangalam family Manoj Dayaram
Manuel Castro Manuel Meyer Manzi Mara Donahoe Marc Tetlow Marcel Botha
Marci Howdyshell Margaret Bronson Margaret Nguyen Margaret Steinbrink
Margaretha Finefrock Margie Meier-Belt Margie Zeidler Mari Sasano Maria B. Mayer
Maria Finley Maria Fisher Maria K. Campolongo Maria Pereda Maria Tsoukalas
Maria Uriela Moreno :) Mariah Erlick Mariah Kelly Mariah Olson marianhd.com
Marianne P. Marianne Zielke Marie Cosgrove-Davies Marie Hohner Marie Kieronski
Marie Lamb marie landry Marie Lynn Wagner Marie-Caroline Vidican
Marie-Pier Remillard Marika Collins Marilyn Kontz Mario Breitbarth Marisa J. Lown
Marisol Romero Marissa Finn Marissa Mann Marissa Perez Marjorie Gelin Goodwin
Mark and Liz Wilson Mark and Pam Grimes Mark AR Thompson Mark Ashley Mark Fadden
Mark Gillan Mark Ivey Mark Jurisch Mark L. Rosenberg Mark P. Griffin Mark Perkins
Mark the Encaffeinated One Mark Yates Mark Zebley Markj Marko Max Radosevic Marla
Marlene Vazquez Marmæl Marquis and Jaime Marquise Lee Martha Vallon Martin
Martin Adler martin shaw Martine Vijn Nome Martins Rungainis Márton Juhász
Marty McGuire Marty Otto Mary and Ben Mullen Mary and Jon Gerush Mary Au
Mary Ball Mary Beth Decker Mary Beth Herring Mary Byington Mary Catherine Augstkalns
Mary Gandolfo Mary Gray Hutchison Mary Lehman Mary Paige Mary Purpura
Mary Sprowles Mary Stack Mary Tweedie Mary Zamboldi Marylou Millard Ferrara
Mat Elmore Mathias Søderlund Mathieu ~|||< Bergeron Mathieu C. Matie Trewe
Matilda Clarke Matt Bell Matt Gannon Matt Harker Matt Hartley Matt Horowitz
Matt I. Matt McGlincy Matt Moretti Matt Ritt Matt Smith Matt Wang
Matt, Selena, and Jodi Matthew Begley Matthew Cadrin Matthew D Matthew J. Huie
Matthew Legault Matthew McCurdy Matthew Miller Matthew S. Matthew Stewart
Matthew Zdinak Matthias Armbruster Matthijs van den Berg Maureen Cooke Maureen S.
Maurice Evans Maurice FitzGerald Maurice Samulski Max Klass Max Licker max thiede
Max Torres Maxime Lacombe Maximilliano Zazillie May Kirby McCue family
Meagan and Brian Molnar Meagan Gravelle Meaghan Meaghan Whalen
Meeka and David Simerly Meftihe Meg B Meg Duarte Meg Rudge Megan Bowes
Megan Case Megan Cross Megan Izarra Megan McLeod Megan Smith Megan Todd
Meghan Dixon, RD Meghan Higginbotham Meghan Lundrigan megosh Melanie Bailey
Melanie Bass Pollard Melanie Freisinger Melanie Palevich Melissa and Michelle Stocker
Melissa Boren Melissa Friedman Melissa Galliher-Hay melissa ilana cohen Melissa Johnson
Melissa Krause Melissa Makfinsky Melissa Mattenson Hack Melissa Powell Melissa Rudolf
Melissa Spencer Melita Savona Melmar Melody Baker Melody Lemonds mhaire fraser
Micah and Susan Maziar Micah Baclig Michael "Hardcore" Gaultois Michael Alexander Gonser
Michael Alparan Michael and John Michael Barendregt Michael Beezley Michael Brassell
Michael Cooney Michael D. Jolliffe Michael Davis Michael Gellar Michael H Bullington
Michael Hammer Michael Harper Michael Henderson Michael Hernandez Michael J. Salhany
Michael Jackson Michael Janz Michael Koch Michael Leibel Michael Nand
Michael R. Lupacchino Michael Schaefer Michael Shaw Michael Swain Michael Taschuk
Michael Van Dyke Michael Verrilli Michael Woitzek Michal Story Michala Kazda
Michel Molinier Michele Cormier and Christine Langill Michele E Michele Tremblay
Michele Verduchi Michelle and Amanda Quintanilla Michelle Arrowood Michelle Bar-Evan
Michelle Brunke Michelle D'Amico Rosenthal Michelle Douglas Michelle Laughran
Michelle Melcher Knight Michelle Mullins Michelle Parks Michelle Peet and Rex Robinson
Michelle Plyem Michelle Quenneville Michelle Spatafora Michelle Wang
Michigan Therapeutic Consultants Miguel Mejia Mike Mike and Abra Henry, State College PA
Mike and Mary Johnston Mike Barnard Mike Battles Mike G. Mike Laidlaw Mike Lewelling
Mike Milius Mike Moore Mike Munsil Mike Otto Mike Skolnik Mike Sullivan
Mikhail Vaysman Millie Mrvica Mimi Wright Mina Tran Mirelle Blassnig Miri Mogilevsky
Miss Cole Miss Sable Mitch Gustav the Robot Mitch Mayhon Mitchell G. Mithilesh Ranganna
MJ Manna Mk Mollie and Jason Molly A. B. Molly C. Molly Hunker Molly Kalan
Mom Mona Fosheim Øwre Monica J. Johnson Monica Ng Monica Zawicki Monika Owens
Monique Boustani Monique Mooney Montalvo family Moops Moozlers Morandia
Morgan Daven Morgan Truax Mori-sama Moritz Hoffmann Mr Paul David Hill
Mr. and Mr. Agnew Mr. Bucky Mr. Crawley Mr. Kennedy Mrs. E. K. Cook Ms. Priscilla Lim
Mujtaba Al-Qudaihi Mukethe Kawinzi Mustafa Mert Metin mwk My Darling Mother Deborah
My dear friend, Mariann Nagy Mycroft Myra Oltsik N. Varma N.Chambers Nadia Bruno
Nadine F. Nana Brunk Nancy Burgus Nancy Elizabeth White Nancy Guthrie Nancy Petru
Nanner Naoise Golden Santos Naomi Black naomi dagen bloom Naomi Novik
Napril Halzke Narguess Noshirvani Natalia Estrada Natalie Novacek Natasha Smith
Nate Allen Nate and Abby Collins Nathalie de Graauw Nathan "The Nate" Murphy
Nathan and Larissa Green Nathan and Milica Nathan and Natalie Nathan Bueche
Nathan Howell Nathan Klatt Nathan Reinhart Nathan Venturini Nathan Windsor
Nathanael Rosenheim Nathanlel Senff Neal Gorenflo Neelam Amin Neil Brock Neil Miller
Nelda Mays NETGOALIE Neve Gignilliat Nhonami Nibbler Seifert Nicholas Boyd
Nicholas Clark Nicholas Harman Nicholas Hendley Nicholas Leeman Nicholas Tam
Nichole Simmons Nick and Marie West Nick and Wendy Bresnyan Nick Arango
Nick Garland Nick Hildenbrandt Nick Jackson Nick P nick shin Nick Tekverk
Nick Wolfe nickawanna shaw Nicki Jimenez Nico e Bastien Nico Tombo!
Nicoel Mitchell-Duff Nicola Mazbar Nicole B. Nicole Flam
Nicole Groeneveld, for my son Isaac: food stamps help end domestic violence Nicole J. Dunn

Nicole Schtscherbina Nicoletta Laing Nicolle Woods Niffer J Nigel Heid-Malina Nikki and Jim Stevens Nikki Wall Nikolaus Stein Nikolette and Kris Bennett Nina Cary Ning Bao Noah Shelton Noel and Nancy Talcott Noel Stave Noelle Bittner Nonsensical Jellyfish Noreen O'Brien Norm North Brooklyn Farms Nupi Nuria Baldello-Sole nVitius Obafemi Babatunde Oluwasanu Ayotomiwa Oso Ogul Thorbull Kafinski Oier Marigil Zaldua Olddreamer Olivia Gerhard Olivia Spencer Olivier A. Olivier Biwer Oopah OreoKat Oscar and Agnes Gardner Oskar Simann Otter Abrahamson Owl Peak Farm Foundation P Deaton P.G. Giannini Pablo Varela Paige Conley Paloma Baytelman Pam Adams Pam Misener Pam Patrick Pam Washburn Pamela J. Kemp pamela klinger Pamela Lindsey Pamela RW Kandt Pamela Smith Devine Pao Franco Parsley Pascal Blunk Pat "maybe now I'll try cooking" MaherPruden Pat Aderhold Pat Y Rudolph Patrice Fowler Patricia A. FitzGerald Patricia Bradshaw Patricia Jenatsch Patrick A. Martin Patrick Bateman Patrick Dapolito Patrick Gage Kelley Patrick Schott Patrick Scott Patrick Van de Casteele Patrick Weir Patti Kaech-Feder Patti Thompson Patton Planning Patty Harrison Patty Welch Paul and Ashleigh Todd Paul and DeAnn Iatesta Paul Blankinship Paul DeLaVergne Paul Eder Paul Egan Paul Freelend Paul J Thordarson Paul K Penney Paul Lim Paul Miller Paul Popernack Paul Schleicher Paul W. Moore Paula Ceballos Paula Gehrig Paulette Pauline and Vinnie Gaudio PE-ACE Peace Love Plates Pearlyn Lii Pedro Rosário Silva Peg G Peggy M Jordan Penny A Penny Fuller Percy Swint Perian Sully Pete and Clare Pete Delahunty Pete Salas Jr Peter Capozzi Peter Lu Peter McLean Peter McQuillan Peter Nelson Peter Stalder Peter, Calgary, Canada Petr Shchepilov Phil White Philip Burn Philipp Dörfler Philippe Debar Phinxy Phoebe Seiders Phoenixphire24 Phuong Ngo Pia Bloom Pia Marshall Pidor Pieface Pierce Graham-Jones Pierre Jean Leonard Pierre Mobian Pierre-Luc Ping-Fen Hsu Pinkie Ector Po-An Shen Poonam Basu Price Murry Priscilla Lotman Prism Bucket Pritika Gulliani Jain ProgramCat Proper Soda PS Ecker Queen Katicus Quincy Clark Quinn Connolly Quinn DuPont R. Bowen R. Crane R. Gilmore Rachael Manto Rachael Pratt Rachel and Justin Hannon Rachel and Justin Proffitt Rachel Blum Rachel Carlin Rachel Cusick Rachel Kronowitz Rachel Ma rachel wagner Rachel Ward Rachel Warren Rachel Wilson Rachele F Gilman Rachele Nader Rachie Loni RACoomer Rado Volny Raelyn Rafael Jimenez Rafael Slonik Raffer Rahmin Sarabi RailDr Raise Your Rainbow Raiza Rin Ralph Gorin Ramla N. Gabriel Ramon Quesada Randy Thompson Raoul Kim raphzore Rasmus Brøndsted Rasmus Wriedt Larsen Raúl "borfast" Santos Ray Andrews Ray Barilaro Ray Doeksen Ray Tomlin Rayan Bouajram Rayna Mayer Realizing Empathy Rebecca and Michael Lane Rebecca Ann Coles Rebecca Bright Rebecca Brightly Rebecca Clarizio Rebecca Curran Rebecca D Nichols Rebecca Goldman Rebecca Gottlieb Rebecca Levitan Rebecca McDougall Rebecca Palm Rebecca Siegel Jones Rebecca Smith Rebecca Tarby Rebecca Vendetti Rebecca Waldman Rebekah Bennetch Rebekah V Swanson reCAP Mason Jars Regina Castillo Reginald G. H. Rutherford Rémi Webster Rémy Donahey Rena Greene Renae Slaton RENDER: Feminist Food & Culture Quarterly Renea Hanna, hello-darlin.com Renee Wu Rev. Teresa Wayman Rev. Thomas Hoffmann Reva Corrigan Rhanee Wilkinson Rhian I'Anson Eastham Rhiannon Pelagia Lewis Rhys Fowler Rian Curley Ricardo Bohn Rich Gladwell Rich Shipley Rich Vreeland Richard Richard Duck Richard George III Richard Lecours and Kathryn Penwill Richard Libera Richard Murray Richard Perkins Richard Thomas Richard Woodruff Rick Mason Rick Schumacher Rickey Hodinh Ricky Ma Rik Ditter Riley L. Rita E. Williams Roast Finkel Rob and Christina Squires Rob Derstadt Rob Johnston Rob Levy Rob Marin Rob Miga Rob Nero Rob Newell Rob Reay Rob Robertson Rob Weir Robb Wynn Robbin Jones Robert Boylan Robert D L Brown Robert E. Stutts Robert Epps Robert Evans Robert Gates Robert Hovey Robert MacGillivray Robert Rodgers Roberto M. Merza III Robin Baird Robin M. Glenn Robin Yang Robin-Ann Klotsky Rocio Petersen Rodney MacDonald Rohan de Silva Roma Romany Redman Romi Ron and Cindy Thompson Ron Cuirle Ronald Koo Ronda Simpson Ronda Sly-Jones Ronda Stevenson RonnieB Ronny Nunez rosa Rosalie Marshall Rosano Rose Rose Abdoo Rose Bouthillier Rose de Mars Rose Gwiniolen Rose Ludwig Rose Wu Rosie-pants Ross Givens Rossana Robinson Roxanne Cheney Roxanne Daniels Roxanne Sutton Roy McElmurry RTS Rubaiya Islam Rubek and Irene Rumian Rusinowicz family Russell Brown Russell Loud Russell Martinez Rustle the Love Muscle Ruth Ann Hummel Ruth Crump Ruth Gutman Ruth J. Kotsalos Ruth Waddell and Eric Stockel Ruthie Wharton Ryan "Windcatcher" Frayne Ryan and Kate Ryan Berger Ryan Boucher Ryan Canty Ryan Carlson Ryan Creed Ryan E Cummings Ryan Edgerley Ryan Hall :) Ryan Kish Ryan Link Ryan P Kilby Ryan Roth Ryan T. Miller Ryan Thomas Moriarty S. Gilbert S. Henderson S.C. Mirabal S&C Hautz Sabrina Strauss Saffron and Kumquats Sagetribe Sahar Sally Almquist Sally Bozzuto Sally Culver Sally Poulsen Salomea Salon on 5th Sam and Rebecca Lawrence Sam Ellens Sam James Sam Klein Sam Maloney, @sam0ny Sam Wakefield Samantha Elghanayan Samantha Park Samantha Sheppard Sameer Sammi Smith Lelliott Sammy Samuel Heinsohn Samuel Vlasta Samuel Yu Samwise Crider Sandara Ros Sande Chisholm Sandeep Ajith Sandra Grady Sandra Hoshooley Sandra L. Doggett Sandra Roddy-Adams Sandra74 Sandro Menzel Sandy Sandy Behler Sandy Brown Sandy Valois Sandy, Emma, and Anna Sang Sang Lee Santiago Martinez Vara Sara Garver Sara Glick Sara Kimes Sara Mueller Sara Saljoughi Sara Schamber Sara Speer Selber Sara Star Sara Stroman Sara Thompson Sara Torello Hart Sarah Ackerson Sarah and Jason Sarah and Tim Mardon Sarah and Tyler Sarah Blackstock Sarah Brewer Sarah Dunifon Sarah E. Ward Sarah Ellen Bautista Sarah Elmaleh Sarah Forrestal and Peter Lee Sarah Gatien Sarah Gregson Sarah Heering Sarah Heile Sarah Hernandez Sarah Howard Sarah J. Christensen Sarah JRP Sarah L. Green Sarah Lewis Sarah Mahoney Sarah McIntyre Sarah Parga Sarah Parsons Sarah Perry Sarah S. Sarah Salimi Sarah Troedson Sarah Tunnell Sarah Walz Sarah, Vanko, and Oliver Saralee R. Leary Sarngsan Riewchotisakul, Tone Sati Suwinski Savage Health Savannah and Isabella Hoy Saxon Royale Weber Scot and Corey Scott Bryson Scott Cosgrove Scott Hoerner Scott Loonan Scott M Scott Neilson Scott S. Semester Scott Szyjewicz Scott VanVossen Sean Abley Sean Hou Sean Johnson Sean Lavender Sean O'Regan Sean Shanahan Seasoned with Chaos, a blog on food and family Sebastian G Miller Semih Energin Semyon Feldman Seon Augustine Serena Henderson Serge Riou Sergio Hernandez Sergio Olavarrieta Sevigny family Sevone Rhynes Shahin "Shah" Yazdani Shai Keidar Shamhoon Shane Pasley Shannon Gatta Shannon Hammock Shannon James Shannon Name Sharni Ryan Sharon Ann Hagen Sharon Bernard Howard Sharon Chen Sharon Denney Sharon Leung Sharpie Shauna Maldonado Shawn Beard Shawn Craig shawn j Shawn Ligocki Shaynna Gueno Shayonna Cato Shazia, Ovi, and Mini Malik Sheila Ford, MSN, RN, CNL Shellee and Allen Chen Shelley A. Shelley B. Shelley Cao

Shelley Embrey Shelley Ollig Shelley Pitts Shelly Krotine Sherene Azar Sherri Sherri M Sherrill Sherry Sherry Lester Sherwin Fong Shingo Nishimura Shirley Tong Shley the Yellow Dart Sid and Kat Sidhartha Gautama Sih Yu Chen-Found Silly Chicks Prepared Foods Silver Denton Silvie SimJoSt Simon Engqvist Simon Goodman Simon Kwak Simon Leblanc Simon Matthee Simona Bot Simone Simone Cosma Sinclair Browning Sinclair Laursen SK Gaski Slaine Fullerton Smiley family Snipe Soil2Soul Solveig Kurowski Someone from PowerUp Ethiopia Sondra Veldey Song Hia Songsit Kodee - Gibson Sonia Murray Sonia R. Martinez Sonrisa Sonya Stewart-Wright Sophie Yu Soujanna Sarkar Spencer Stewart Spencer Vaughn Spice Runner SpongeBob SquarePants SPROUT Stacey Goguen Stacey Wong Stacie Nagy Stacy Bloom Stacy Hyder Combest Stacy Meppen Stacy Rogers Sharp Stacy Wolberg Stan Yamane Stanley Thomas Stavros Nikos Stavros Stef H. Stefan Loble / Bluff Works Stefania Dunaway Stefannie Toth Steffen Kaupp Stella Au Stella Runkle Stephanie A. Cain Stephanie A. Williamson Stephanie Duchin Stephanie Ewen Stephanie Gerbracht Stephanie Harper Stephanie Hogan Stephanie K Cox Stéphanie Laroche-Pierre Stephanie Liu Stephanie M. Urch Stephanie Marchello Stephanie Myrie Stephanie Rogus Stephanie Sturm Stephanie Terry Stephanie Thoe Stephanie Van Dyk Stephen Stephen Fols Stephen Gibbon Stephen Lord stephenallenjrlaw Sterling Swigart steve Steve :) Steve and Marsha Taylor Pepper Steve Bowcutt Steve C Lee Steve Farmer "The Blue Saint" Steve Faulkner Steve Feng Steve Hallman Steve Huynh Steve Katz Steve Kimball Steve Ling Steve Pinkham Steven Steven Bowley Steven Chen Steven Earl Steven Gatlin Steven Ginsberg Steven Goldman Steven Johnson Steven Olender Steven Tate Stevie Rae Fure Stewart McTavish Stewart Yu Stijn Verdickt Stitch Storm Cowle Stretch Recipes, Inc. Stuart Suburban Jubilee Sue Clinnick Sue Dempsey Sue Hartman Sue Stoessel Sukumar Ramanathan Sulayman Bimar Summer Page Susan and Al Averbach Susan Beil Susan Brennan Susan Bryan Susan Collins Susan Coppenrath Susan Crow Goldstein Susan Finkelman Susan Foulds Susan Gauthier Susan Gilbert Susan Gordon Susan M Brown Susan M. Diliberti Susan Nordstrom Susan O. Susan Prion Susan Rack Susan Silbermann Susan W. Susan Worthington Susana Machado, RNc-OB SusanJ Susanna Griffith Susieclouds Suzannah Schneider Suzanne Suzanne H. Hooper Suzanne Liebergen Suzanne O'Dell Suzanne Samson Suzanne St Thomas Suzanne Sutton Suzanne Thomas Sybil Turner Sydney Shillieto Sydney Thompson Sylvanye "Sam" Roh Sylvia Abney Sylvia and Lorenz Gabriel Flores Szymon Wilczek T Alphin t gaines T. C. McGarrigle T.R. Tabitha Boyer Taco Boy Tadeu Banzato Takahiko Fujita Tal Milner Talavera family Talen DM Johnson Talia Ralph Tamanna Tammy Tammy Lee Tamzen Tan Bro Tankooni Tanya Luthin Tapasvi Sehgal Tara Bloyd Tara C Harrison Tara Shakespeare Beamesderfer Tara VanDenheuvel Tasha Bachand Tatiana Reyes Jove Taverna Alessio, Udine Taylor Colon Taylor J. Snider Taylor Kearney Taylor Maltz Teal Pfeifer Team Crazy Town Team Elliott tedder Teresa Tereza Bazac Terra A Jones Terri Lovins Terri Lynn Almeda Terry cedrone Tess R. Ornstein Tessa Williams Thanh Tan Thank you God The Almquist-Houston family The Baluk family The Bowen family at Meadowdale Farm The Burner The Canucks Upstairs The Clancy Clan The Clinic, Phoenixville PA (Free Medical Clinic) The Color Blue, and the Letter M The Comport family The Contreras family The Crumpacker Smith family The Danzigers The DiBenedetto family The Fix-it Sisters The Flahertys The Fleck family The Greenhouse family The Grillo family The Hall family The Honors Academy of Literature, Reno NV The Idiot Economist The Intrieri family The Jegier family The Kelly Girls The Kellys in Cowtown The Kilgore family The Leonard family The McKinley family The Neumans The Nuanii The O'Donovans The Palmers The Phair family The Posnick family The Pruitt family The Roberts family The Sciaino family The Shaw family The Sheriff of Mars documentary The Slyter family The Sriracha Cookbook The Stoddard family The Thompson family, Naperville IL The Tow family The Wagner-Wangs The Warr The Welsh-Buck family Theresa Clonts Theresa Landell Theresa Marth Thomas and Sarah Mcdaniel-Dyer Thomas Dickert, DC Thomas Nemeth Thomas Parrillo Thor Olavsrud Tian Mu Tifany Ness Tiffany Adams Tiffany Brown Olsen Tiffany Kelly Tiffany Nesson Tiffany Poe, CEC Tiffany Tia Montano Tiffany Topol Till tim elliott, heathcliff13 Tim Hickey Tim Jordan Tim Round Tim, Jaime, and Cooper Philips Timothy Mekhlin Timothy O'Dell, Corinth VT Timothy T. Deeter Timothy Vander Ploeg Tina E Poley Tina Panteleakos Tina Smith Tiny House Project Charleston Titousensei Tizzy Lockman Tk Appleton tk knowles Toby and Isaac Todd Sattersten Todd Taylor Todd Tucker Tom Anderson, Newport Beach Tom Bantle Tom Mawn, III Tom Mills Tom Shen Tom W Davis III Tom Wedell Tomarah Joyner Tomaso P. Tommy Dore tommy howell-owasso Tommy R. Pendergrast Tonia Yoder Tony Pangilinan Torin Reed Tracey Ledel Traci Tracy Challis Tracy Dawicki Tracy F. Tracy Hodson Tracy Hug Tracy Murray Tracy Nguyen Tracy Plyem Tramp Press, Ireland Travis Espinoza Trent Petersen Trevor Arat Trevor Sheldon Tricia and Craig Russ Tricia Jackson Tricia Noble Trina Blake Trinity Episcopal Church, Toledo OH Trish Lobenfeld Troy Hill Tswm Vang turtle Tye Johnson Tyler Tyler and Ali Savage Tyler Goblin Tyson Thompson Ukeme Umana Urban Oasis Project, Miami FL V J Webb VA Nguyen Valerie and Dean Lefor Valerie Ingram Valerie Taylor Valery Federici Valslide Vanessa Lynn Weathers Vanessa Oliver Vanessa Regan Varelie Venia, organizedbites.com Venki Das Vera S. Ocampo Vera Salvisberg Veronica M. Veronica Newton Vertti Vic Fryzel Vickey Power Vicki Chan Victor Almgren Victor Freitas Victoria Hoyt-Heydon Victoria Martinez Victoria Wilson Victoria Wojcik Vidya Kapadia Vincenzo Urbisci Virginia Murphy Virginia Wohltmann Visalachy Sittampalam Vlad Dragusin Vladimir Sabajo Vuttirat Sangkorntanakij Walt Wanda Jean Warren Dane Warren Kuo Waylon Wolf Black Wei-Hsin Chen Wenda M. Friesner Wendi A. Dunlap Wendy Nevett Bazil Wendy Stephens Wes "Captain Fun" Wilson Weslyn Wiley Whitney J Wadlow Whitney Moses Wilbur Steinhaus Wiley Not Coyote WIll Andrews Will B. Will Bungarden Willee William Cuff William Hall William Lomica William Luster, MD William Sikkema Wilpe Winnie Chang Wolfi Won June Tai woodfiredpizza.org Woong Chang Worcester Wong family Worrin Wolf Xinyi Gong xtalya Y. Ribiere Yinan Qiu YNWA Yoav Dori Yohan Lefol Yoko Leafchild Takemura Yolanda Reyes Yoon Ha Lee your buddy dom Yukari Yukiko Takiguchi Yulia Korovikov Yurii "Saodhar" Furtat Yusuf Maung Yuta Chiba Yvonne Archer Zach Matthews Zaid Aiman Zakary Mathis Zaphod Beeblebrox Zedd Zen Williams zigzag hotshot Zoë Valette Zombie Squad zurotzu

Index